Stargazing for Beginners

How to Find Your Way Around the Night Sky

Lafcadio Adams

❄ Idle Winter Press
Portland, Oregon

Idle Winter Press
Portland, Oregon
http://IdleWinter.com

First published 2012
Printed in the United States of America

The text of this book is in Adobe Caslon Pro and Helvetica Neue
The constellation diagrams are digitally rendered

ISBN-13: 978-0615757902 (Idle Winter Press)
ISBN-10: 0615757901

Contents

How to Use This Guide

Introduction

This series of stargazing lessons will walk you through many of the constellations visible in the northern hemisphere. Each new lesson will build on information learned in the previous lesson. This is not a reference book for finding a single constellation; it is a step-by-step tutorial for knowing the night sky.

Just as encountering an unfamiliar word within the context of an otherwise simple paragraph is easy to decipher, mastering even a third of the constellations in this guide will sufficiently prepare you to confidently identify unfamiliar constellations on your own using any star chart.

In the Field

For simplicity, the stars in these diagrams are not shown with relative brightness taken into account. When you see the stars in the sky, some will be bright and clear, and some will be very faint. For best results, try to do your stargazing as far away from city lights as you can. Turn off porch lights and other night-vision-destroyers (or block them with your hand as you look at the sky). Choose moonless nights for stargazing. If you bring this guide with you to stargaze, use a light source that is not very bright when you need to refer to the page.

Although spreading out a blanket on the ground to lie on as you stargaze seems like a great idea, often it can be easier to walk around a bit to find all of the constellations you seek, particularly with tall buildings, trees, or hills nearby. A constellation can go from below the horizon to above the horizon if you physically move yourself 50 feet (which will then cause another constellation to dip below the horizon from your perspective). If you spend more than 20 minutes or so stargazing, you can observe the apparent motion of the stars as the Earth spins on its axis—so even if you stay still, stars will dip below the horizon simply because time is passing.

Take Your Time

Identifying constellations is a skill that takes time. Learning to read the sky can be a bit like learning to read words on a page. You'll start by learning one or two, and then one or two more. It's impossible to learn them all quickly, so give yourself some time to learn.

perfectly clear sky:
Stargazing for Beginners:
How to Find Your Way Around the Night Sky

foggy or hazy weather:
Stargazing for Beginners:
How to Find Your Way Around the Night Sky

light sources nearby:
Stargazing for Beginners:
How to Find Your Way Around the Night Sky

Unlike learning to read words on a page, environmental factors come into play each time you stargaze. Not all nights are perfectly clear. Fog, haze, a bright moon, and other light sources can all make constellation hunting seem like trying to read a page without your glasses, or a page with letters and whole words missing altogether. If you struggle on any particular night, know that it is not your fault—just try again on another night or in another location. Also know that eventually these obstacles will no longer be a problem for you as you become familiar with the night sky.

In the example to the left, you can see that if you already recognize the shape of the words "Night Sky," and know approximately where to look for them, you can find them even in unfavorable conditions. If you are just learning how to recognize "Night Sky," unfavorable conditions make it extremely difficult.

As you add more constellations to your repertoire, don't get discouraged if you can't remember all of them or find all of them right away. Quiz yourself every time you're outside on a clear night, and don't be too hard on yourself. Go back to the beginning (or back one or two lessons) as often as you need to.

For best results, proceed through the lessons in order. You may return to previous lessons to refresh your knowledge, but skipping ahead may be difficult—each lesson builds on knowledge from the previous lesson.

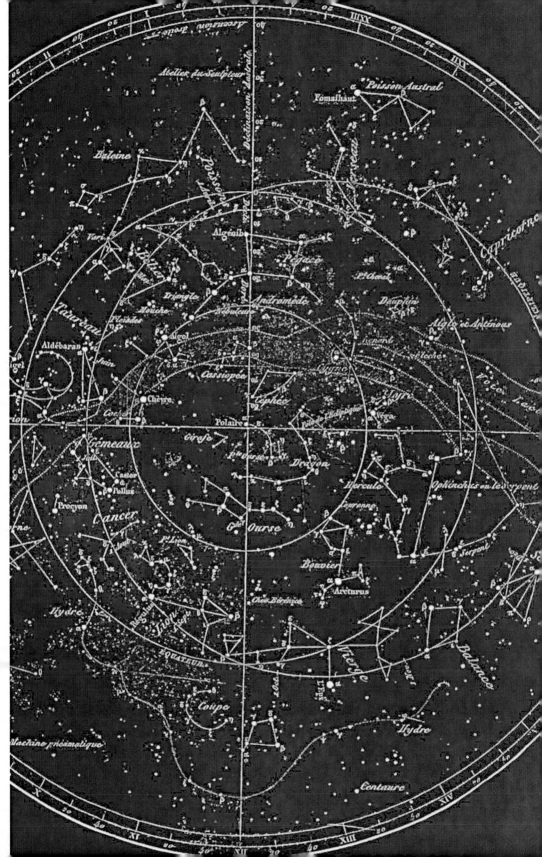

Lesson 1:
The North Star

Prerequisite

As it turns out, you have to start somewhere, so there's a prerequisite for this course:

Find the Big Dipper yourself.

If you don't already know it when you see it in the sky, have someone point it out to you. If you're in the northern hemisphere, it should always be above the horizon (as long as you're not too close to tall buildings, tall mountains, or tall trees), and it serves as a good starting place to orient yourself each night.

Become very familiar with the shape of the Big Dipper, and keep working at it until you can always find it, and you're 100% sure that's what you're looking at when you do find it. Once you can do that, you may proceed.

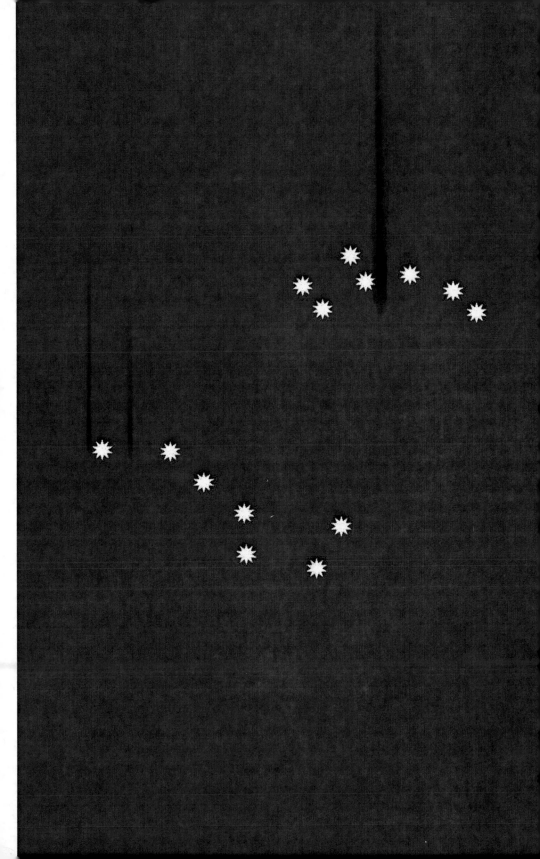

The Big Dipper

The Big Dipper is like a giant frying pan in the sky. Technically, it's not a constellation by itself; it's an "asterism." An asterism is simply a commonly recognizable pattern of stars (the Big Dipper is the lower one in this picture).

The Big Dipper is part of the Great Bear, or Ursa Major. The rest of the stars in Ursa Major are sort of below and to the right of the frying pan, but for our purposes, they're not important. You can use the Big Dipper to find other things in the sky, which is why it's such a good place to start.

Bonus Bits: The middle star in the handle of the Big Dipper is actually 2 stars (well, if you want to get really technical, it's 6 stars). The stars are named Alcor and Mizar, and are sometimes referred to as the "horse and rider." If you look really carefully and have near-normal eyesight, you can actually see two stars very close together. It also helps if it's a really dark, moonless night.

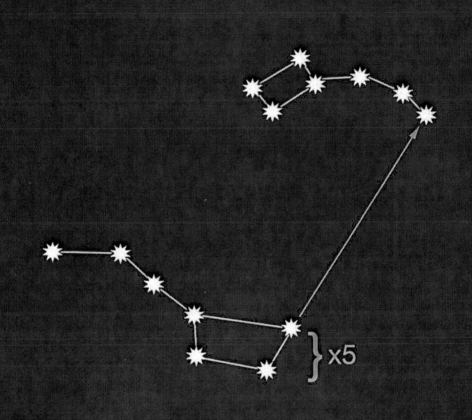

The Little Dipper
and the North Star

The two stars on the front end of the frying pan part of the Big Dipper are called "pointer stars." They point to the North Star, or Polaris. If you take the distance between those stars and extend the line out 5 times that distance, you'll arrive at the North Star.

The North Star is at the tip of the handle of the Little Dipper, or Ursa Minor. The North Star is bright, as are the two stars at the end of the pan of the Little Dipper. The rest are tricky to see unless it's really dark. With bright city lights around, you may only be able to see Polaris and the two stars at the end of the Little Dipper.

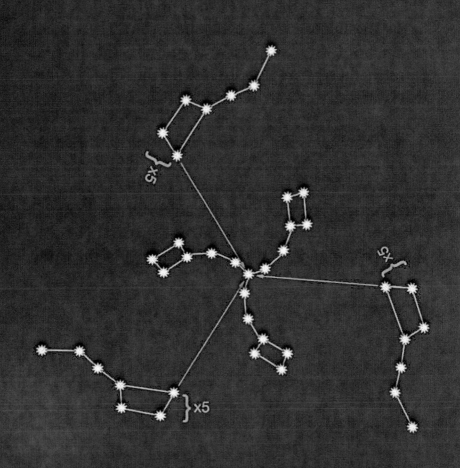

Why Do We Care About Polaris?

The North Star, Polaris, is not a particularly bright star compared to many other stars. The reason we pay attention to it is because it never moves.

It is located directly above the North Pole. As the Earth spins on its axis, the sky appears to rotate (the same way that if you look straight up at the ceiling in your living room while spinning around really fast, the room looks like it's spinning, but it's really you—the North Star is the spot on the ceiling directly above your head).

This diagram shows how the Big Dipper and Little Dipper move throughout the course of the night (and day). The one star at the tip of the handle of the Little Dipper, Polaris, remains in the same spot the whole time. Each night as you begin to stargaze, the stars will be in a slightly different location than the night before (unless you start precisely 4 minutes earlier each night, but pretty soon you'll run into daylight).

Finding the Big Dipper, and using that to find the North Star, will help you find your way around the rest of the sky.

This photograph was taken using a tripod and a 15-minute exposure. During the time the shutter was open, the Earth rotated enough to see a difference in the position of the stars. Polaris appears as a single dot (indicated by the arrow). Other stars close to Polaris advanced just a little bit, and stars farther away show a great deal of motion.

In the full color version of this photograph, it's possible to notice that some of the stars appear to be different colors than others. I'll point out notable blue and red stars along the way as we learn more constellations.

This photograph is called "Continuing Mission," © Daogreer Earth Works.

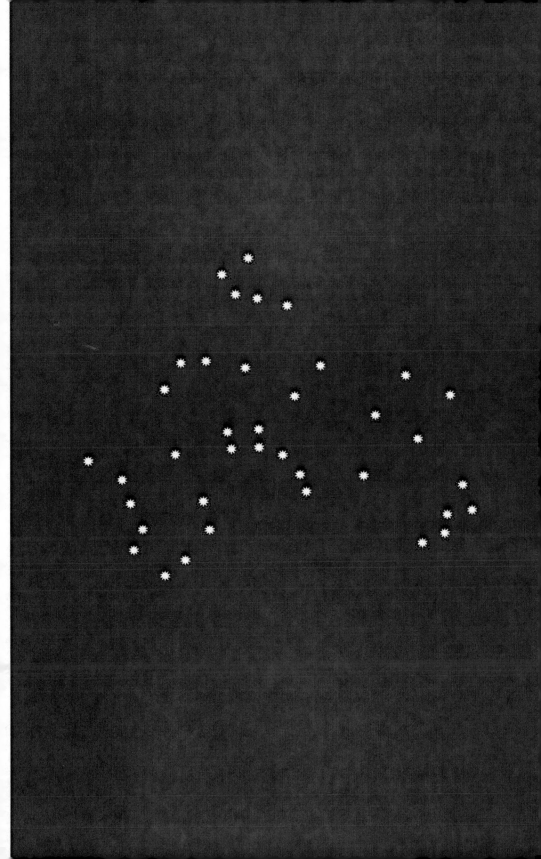

Lesson 2: The Circumpolar Constellations

What Are Circumpolar Constellations?

The North Star, Polaris, is located directly above the North Pole. Other stars in the vicinity are known as "circumpolar," meaning they go in a circle around Polaris. The stars closest to Polaris will always share that region of sky.

Since Polaris will never rise or set, those nearby stars will also be above the horizon most of the time. These are good constellations to become familiar with, because they are always "up" when you want to be stargazing.

Quiz from the last lesson: In the picture to the left, can you find the Big Dipper? Can you use the pointer stars (remember to go 5 lengths out) to find Polaris? How about the Little Dipper?

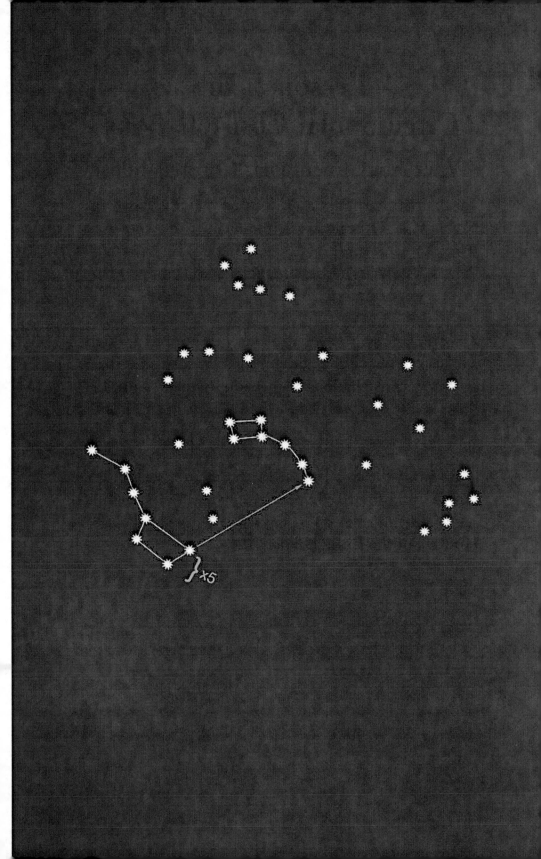

The Big and Little Dippers

Those other stars can be a distraction!

Remember that the stars in these diagrams are not shown with the appropriate brightness. The Big Dipper is made up of very bright stars and will be easier to pick out than the rest of the circumpolar constellations.

Three more circumpolar constellations are shown here. We'll go through them one at a time.

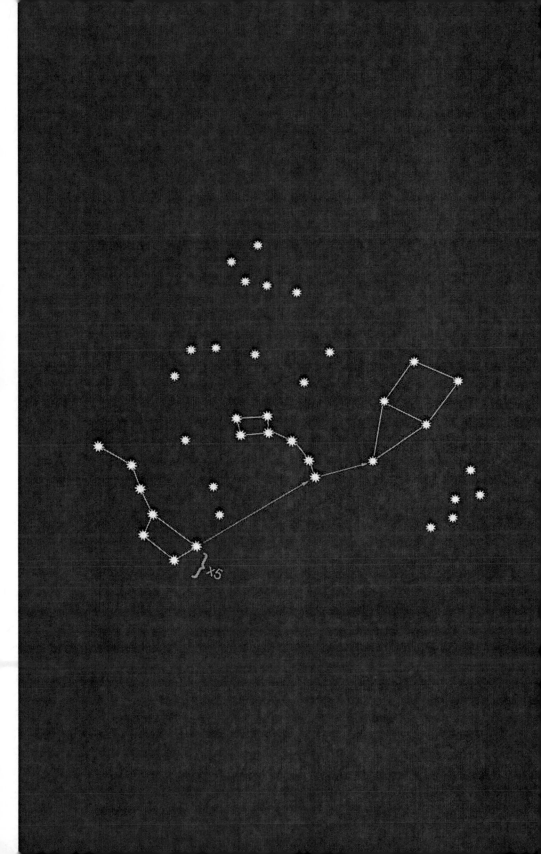

Cepheus, the King

If you use the pointer stars on the Big Dipper to find Polaris, and then keep going, you'll come to the tip of the crown of King Cepheus.

The square is his head, and the triangle is his crown. He's upside-down here.

Cepheus may be a bit tricky to find, as he is composed of mostly fainter stars. Look for him if you are somewhere without much light pollution and no full moon.

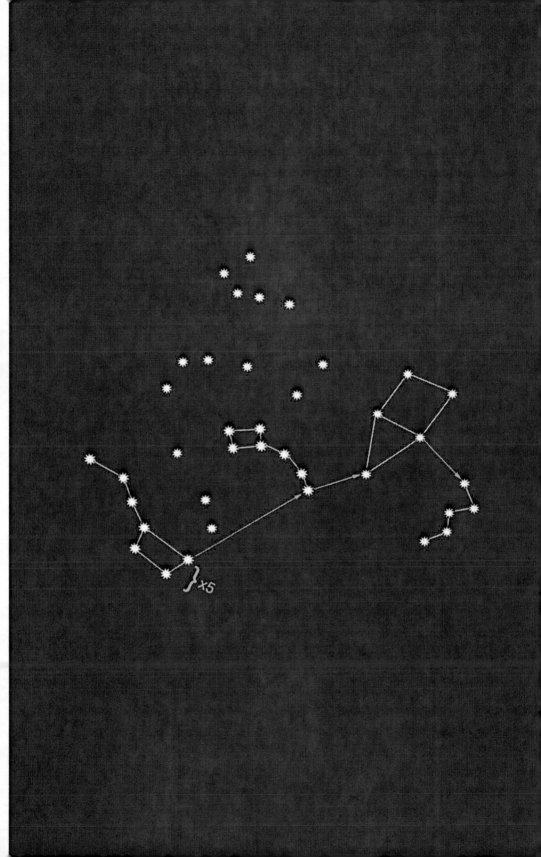

Cassiopeia, the Queen

There are two stars marking where Cepheus's crown meets his face. Cepheus always looks away from the little dipper and toward his wife, Queen Cassiopeia, so the star farther away from the Little Dipper is his eye.

Follow the gaze of Cepheus to Queen Cassiopeia. She looks like an "M" or a "W" in the sky. The shape represents her royal throne, in which she sits admiring herself all day.

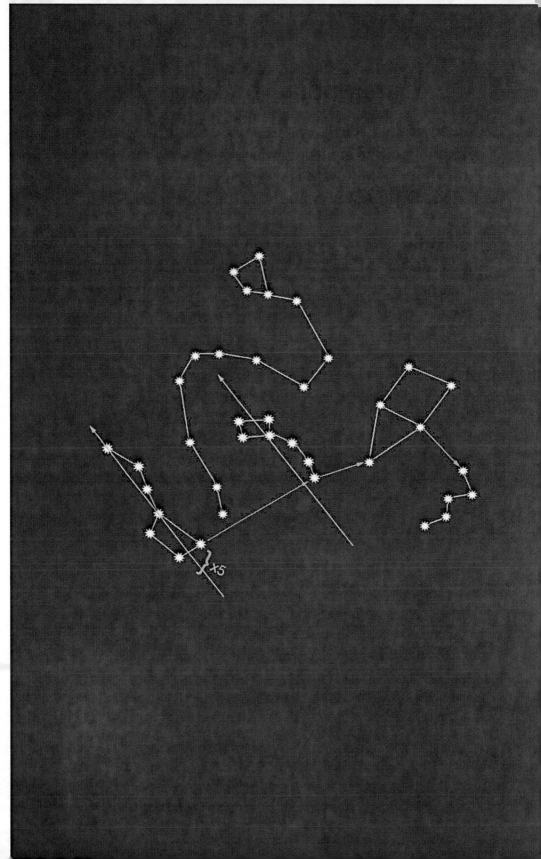

Draco, the Dragon

If you create two roughly parallel lines out of the Big Dipper and the Little Dipper, you'll see a semi-straight line of stars in between. This is the end of the tail of Draco.

Follow it up, and curve around the little dipper, then snake your way up again to find the wonky trapezoid that marks his head. I like to think of Draco as the type of dragon one would find in a Chinese New Year Parade: a head followed by a long, colorful tail.

Lesson 3: Elegant Orion

Prime Star-Watching Time

Now you're familiar with the North Star, and all of its circumpolar friends. Other constellations are far enough away from Polaris to rise and set the same way the sun does.

Star charts are arranged with times of night, hour by hour, and months of the year. That's all well and good for advanced stargazers, but it's a level of complexity unnecessary for the beginner. Let's simplify:

You're most likely to be stargazing from sometime between when it gets dark enough to see all the stars until, let's say... 11:30 p.m., right? I call that "prime star-watching time."

Because of the position of Earth as it orbits the sun every 365 days, different constellations will be overhead during prime star-watching time depending on the season. Constellations visible on a summer night will be "up" during the daytime in the winter, so you won't be able to see them.

The Summer Triangle is a great example of an asterism you can see during the summer. I call those "summer constellations." We'll get to some of those later. For now, we're going to focus on one of my favorite fall / winter constellations, Orion. He'll be most visible during prime star-watching time from October-ish through February-ish.

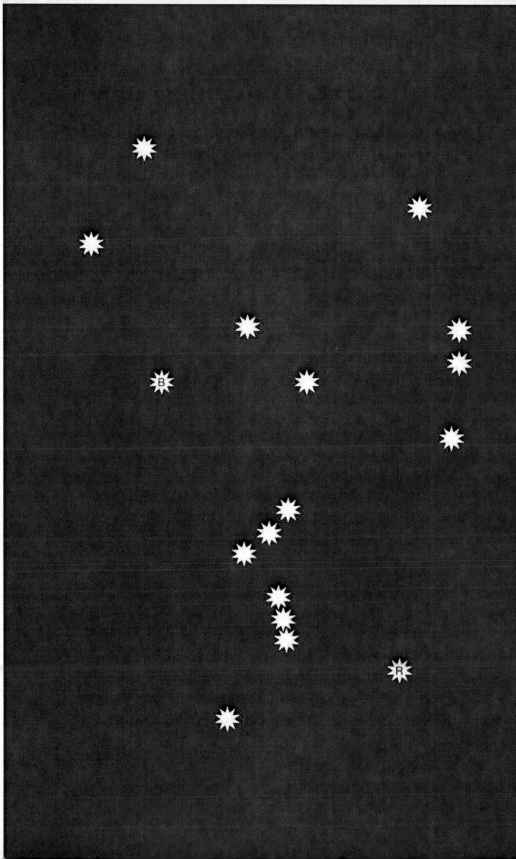

Finding Orion

Find that Big Dipper again. Now turn around, approximately 180°. You should be facing the correct general region of sky.

The picture to the left shows Orion, with just his stars.

A well-known asterism within Orion is his belt. Remember that an asterism is a recognizable group of stars that aren't technically a constellation by themselves. Those three diagonal close-together stars make up the belt, and those stars are the easiest way to find Orion in the sky.

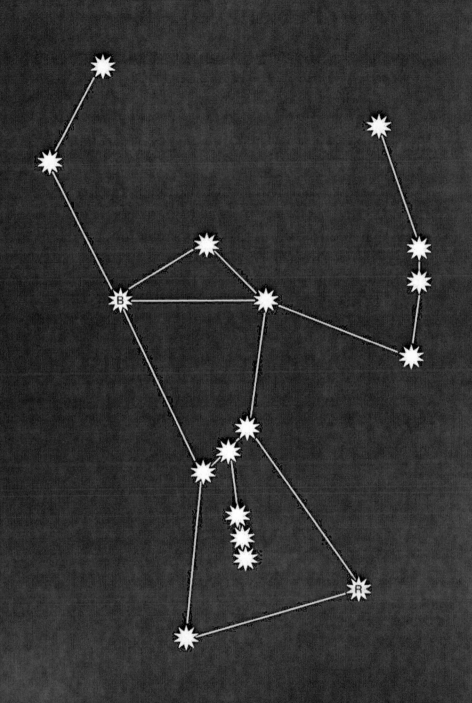

Getting to Know Orion

Orion has several interesting features. Notice that star labeled "R" in the lower right corner? That's actually a blue star. Blue stars are younger, smaller, and hotter than your average yellow star. This one is called Rigel (RYE-jell).

Rigel is around 800 light years away, which means when you see that blue star, you're seeing the light that left Rigel 800 years ago. That sounds incredibly far away, but in the grand scheme of the universe, Rigel is still pretty close to Earth.

Up and to the left (the shoulder opposite Rigel), there's a red star (not RED-red, just kind of pinkish-orange). Red stars are older, larger, and cooler than yellow stars. That one is labeled with a "B," and it's called Betelgeuse (BAY-tell-jooz, or, as almost everyone says, beetle-juice).

Betelgeuse is a red supergiant. It is almost 2000 times the radius of our sun, and could fit within it over 2,000,000,000,000,000 Earths. Betelgeuse is expected to become a supernova sometime in the next million years or so. Because of its distance from Earth, it's possible that it has already done so, but the light from such an event would take hundreds of years to reach us. Orion's other shoulder is a star called Bellatrix.

The dagger hanging from Orion's belt contains a nebula. The middle "star" you see is a nebula made up of dust and gasses, which will eventually condense enough to form new stars. A birthplace for stars is visible from Earth with the naked eye!

Here is an actual photograph of Orion hanging out on the Oregon Coast. Can you find his belt? It's nearly horizontal in this shot. Now find Rigel and Betelgeuse , and the dagger hanging from his belt.

Orion is a hunter. He holds his shield in the arm shown on the right, and a club or sword in the arm that has Betelgeuse as the shoulder. Orion hunts with his two dogs; we'll meet them in the next lesson, but they are visible in this photograph.

This photograph is called "Star Broder," © Daogreer Earth Works.

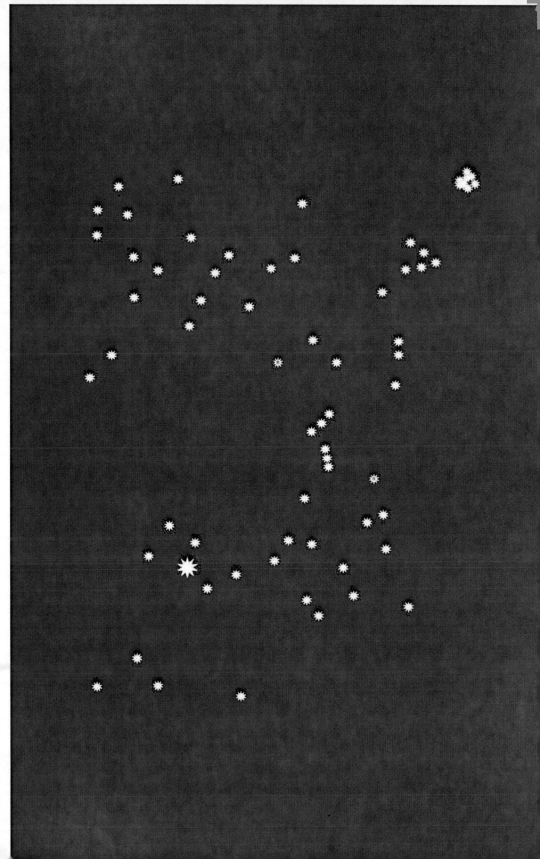

Lesson 4: Ask Orion for Directions

Review from Previous Lessons

The circumpolar constellations rotate in a tight circle around Polaris, the North Star. They are always above the horizon if you're in the northern hemisphere.

Other constellations are farther away from the North Star, and rise and set like the sun. Different constellations will be visible during prime star-watching time (from early darkness to bedtime) at different times of the year.

In the last lesson, we became familiar with Orion. Here he is with some of his closest neighbors. Can you spot him? Look for his belt, and then confirm by finding Rigel and Betelgeuse.

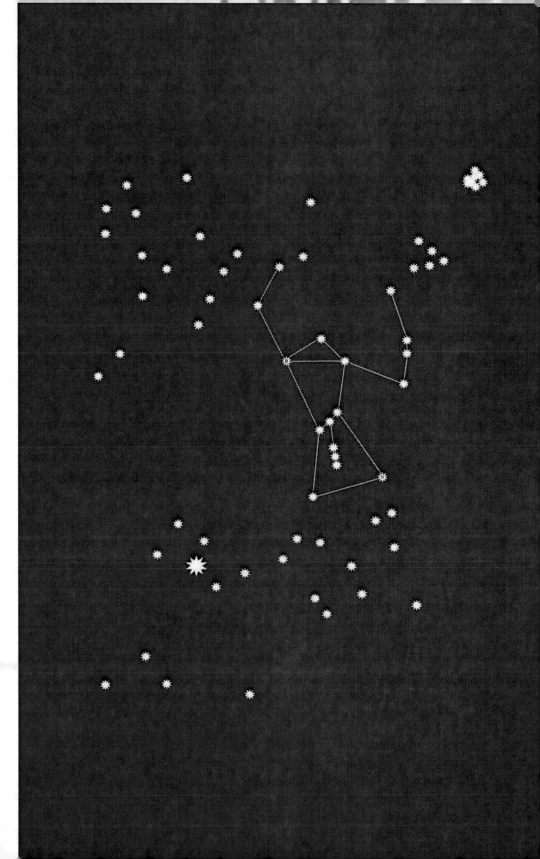

Orion, the Hunter

The stars in Orion can be used to find other constellations nearby, much the same way that the pointer stars in the Big Dipper directed us so effectively toward Polaris.

We can use his belt, his shoulders, his dagger, and Rigel and Betelgeuse to find Canis Major, Canis Minor, Taurus, The Pleiades, Gemini, and Lepus.

That big star you see is the only magnitude difference I'll show, but only because it is the single brightest night-time star. A list of the brightest stars can be found in Appendix A.

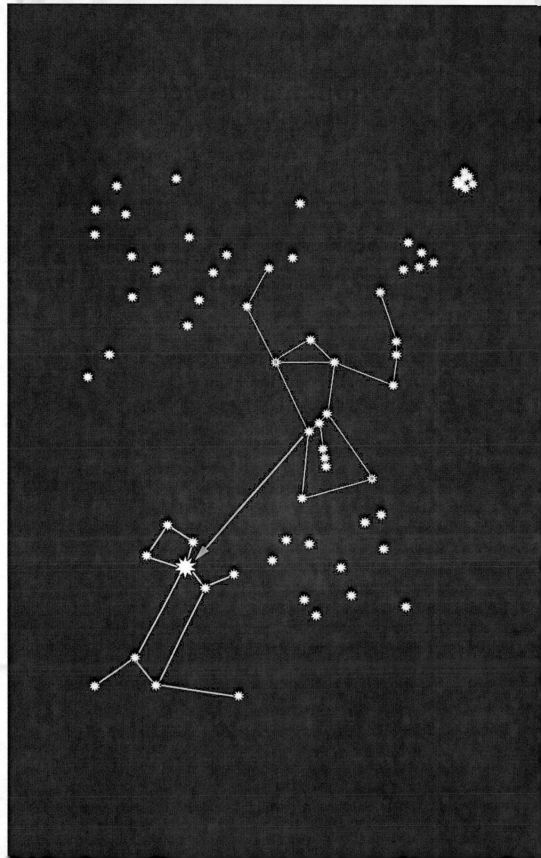

Canis Major, the Big Dog

Follow Orion's belt down to the left. You'll come to a bright star, Sirius (SEE-ree-us; it's a seriously bright star).

It's so bright, in fact, that it's the brightest star you can see from Earth, other than our sun. That makes it the brightest star you can see from Earth at night.

Sirius is the diamond on the collar of Canis Major, or the Big Dog. It is sometimes called the "dog star."

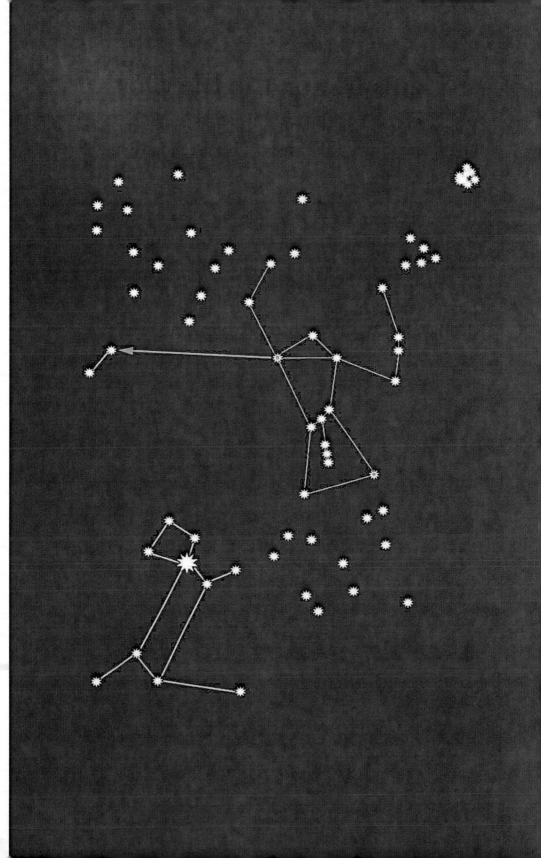

Canis Minor, the Little Dog

Ursa Major (the Big Dipper) is the Great Bear, and Ursa Minor (the Little Dipper) is the Little Bear. It follows, then, that if there is a **big** dog, there should probably be a **little** dog, too (the same logic goes for anything with Northern / Borealis or Southern / Australis in the title, as well).

Follow Orion's shoulders sideways to the left, and you'll come to Canis Minor, or the Little Dog. The Little Dog is just two stars, so it looks more like a hot dog.

The brighter of those two stars is called Procyon (PRO-see-ahn), which is Greek for "before the dog." This is in reference to how the stars rise. You will always see Procyon rise above the horizon before you see the "dog star," Sirius.

Bonus Bits: Canis Minor is one of the 88 modern constellations, but was not recognized by the ancient Greeks. According to the Greeks, Orion had only one dog. Maybe she had puppies.

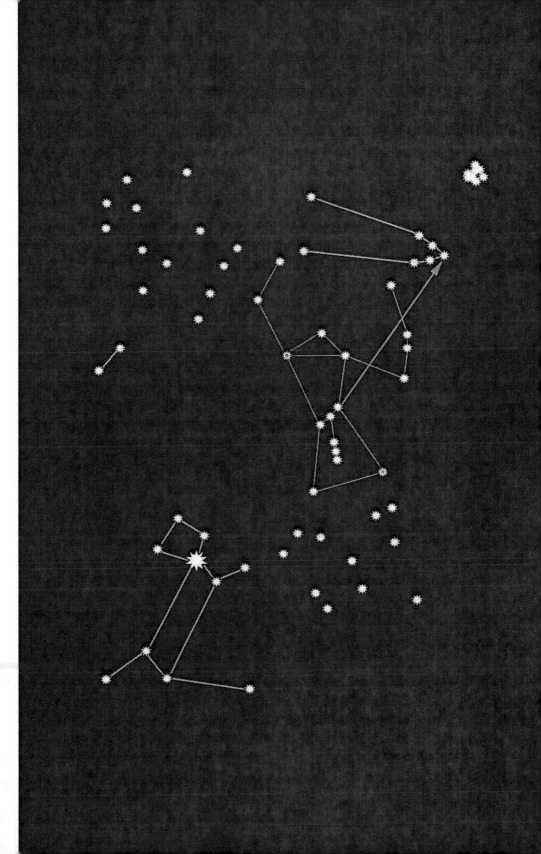

Taurus, the Bull

Follow Orion's belt up to the right, and you'll come to the nose of Taurus, the Bull. Taurus's face is a little V shape, and he has long horns reaching far behind his head.

Taurus has a reddish star, Aldebaran (ahl-DEH-buh-rahn). It's the star closest to the top of Orion's shield (the star that marks the top of the bull's face and the bottom of his horn).

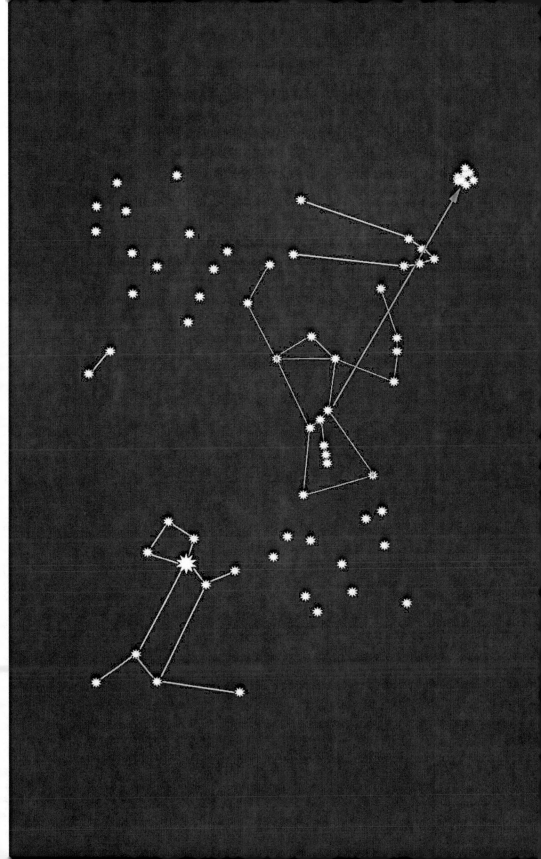

The Pleiades,
or the Seven Sisters

Continue past Taurus until you reach a little blurry patch in the sky. That little blurry patch is a cluster of stars known as the Pleiades, or the Seven Sisters. The cluster is made up of hundreds of stars, currently passing through a dust cloud (hence the blurriness).

Bonus Bits: Most constellations appear the way they do from Earth because of our perspective; if you went to another solar system, they would look completely different. The stars in The Pleiades, on the other hand, are physically near each other in space, so they will look like a cluster from any vantage point.

In Japan, this star cluster is known as Subaru (check the car company logo next time you find yourself near a Subaru).

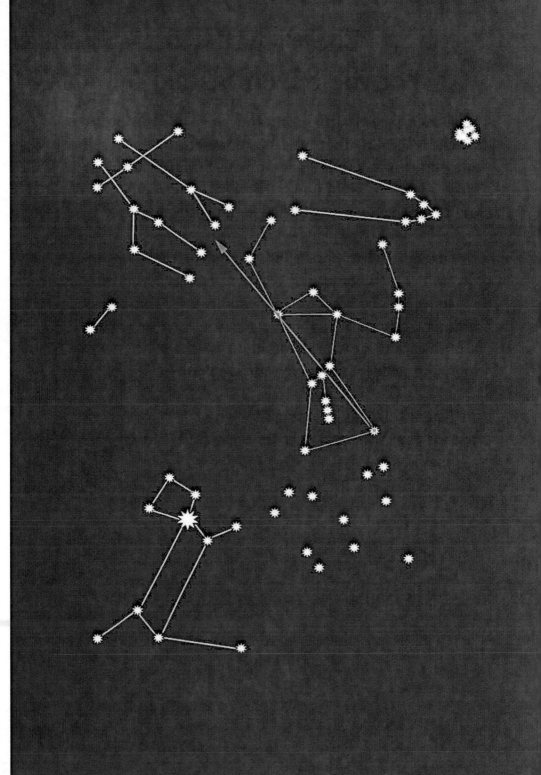

Gemini, the Twins

Draw a line from Rigel to Betelgeuse, and then continue up to Gemini. The stars that make up the heads of the twins are called Castor and Pollux. The head-stars are very bright, and will likely be one of the only recognizable parts of Gemini when you see it in the sky.

Locate the twins carefully! The two head-stars look an awful lot like Canis Minor if you're only going for an approximation. Following the shoulders sideways gets you to the little dog, and the Rigel-Betelgeuse line gets you to the twins. Pollux has really long legs, and Castor has really short legs, so clearly they're fraternal twins.

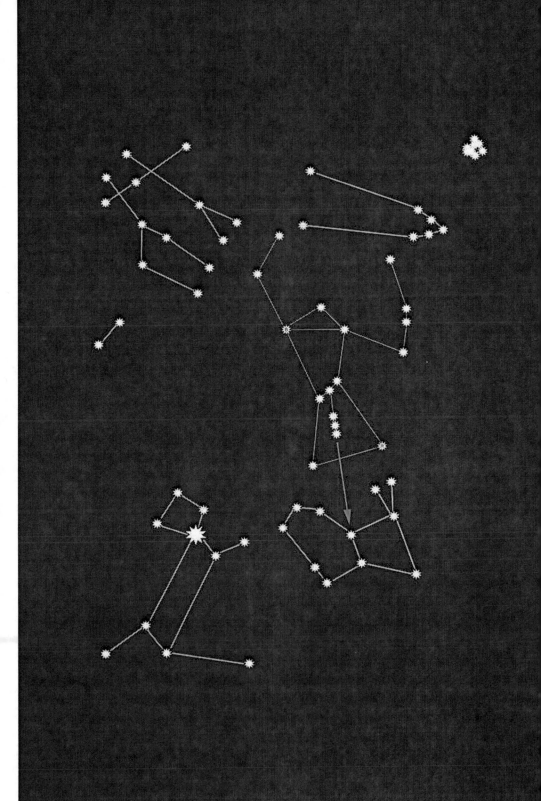

Lepus, the Hare

Shhh! I'm hunting wabbits!

Orion, the hunter, needs some prey, and his dogs like to chase things. Follow his dagger downward to find a rabbit, Lepus.

It's easy to remember the name of this little guy, because rabbits leap-us. Never mind that this gigantic lagomorphic monstrosity could probably take out the Little Dog with one well-placed kick of his non-existent legs...

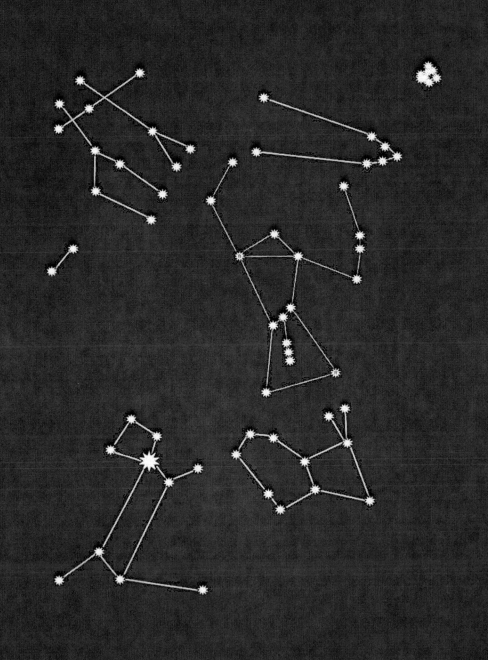

Time to Practice

Now you know all of Orion's neighbors! Let's look once again at the photograph:

Find Orion. Now follow his belt down (to the left) to find Sirius, the bright star on the collar of Canis Major. You can see everything but the tip of the big dog's tail in this photograph.

Follow Orion's shoulders up to the left to find the little dog, Canis Minor.

Follow Orion's dagger down to find Lepus, the hare, just about to dive nose-first into the Pacific Ocean.

If you follow the line between Rigel and Betelgeuse upward, you can get as far as Pollux's toes (he's the long-legged twin), but the head-stars are out of the frame in this shot.

You now have at your disposal two whole patches of sky, and 11 of the 88 constellations, or 12.5% (The Pleiades is considered part of Taurus in the count).

That number becomes even more impressive when you think about all the southern hemisphere constellations you don't have to worry about unless you travel there.

"Star Broder," © Daogreer Earth Works.

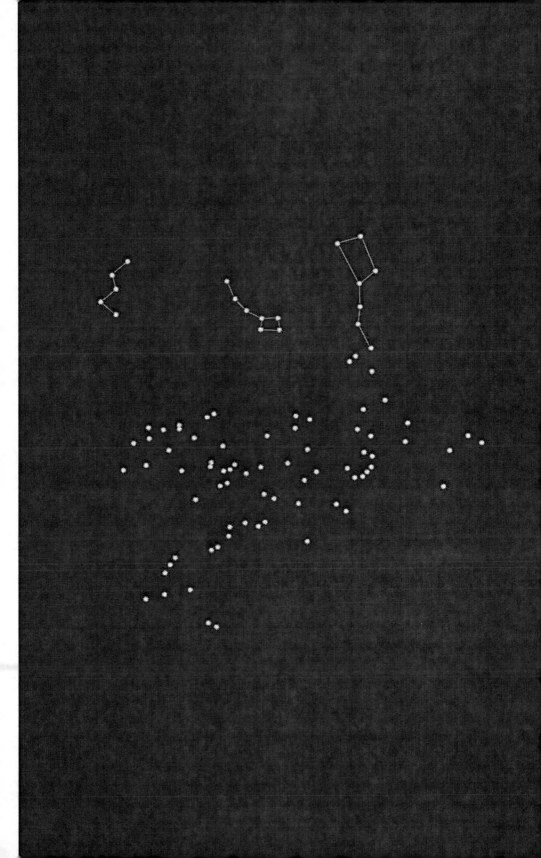

Lesson 5:
Sweet Summer Sky
Wait a While

If you've been practicing along with the real sky, you'll need to wait 6 months between Lessons 4 and 5. I'm sorry about that.

It's summer now, for the purposes of our continuing stargazing education. Most diagrams in this lesson will show both the whole picture (so you can remember where you are), and a zoomed in version so you can see what's going on better.

Start by orienting yourself. Find the Big Dipper, then Polaris, then confirm Cassiopeia.

I've left out Cepheus and Draco, because they're harder to find in the real sky anyway. If you want to quiz yourself a bit more, add them in where you think they should be in your mind, then check yourself by going back to Lesson 2.

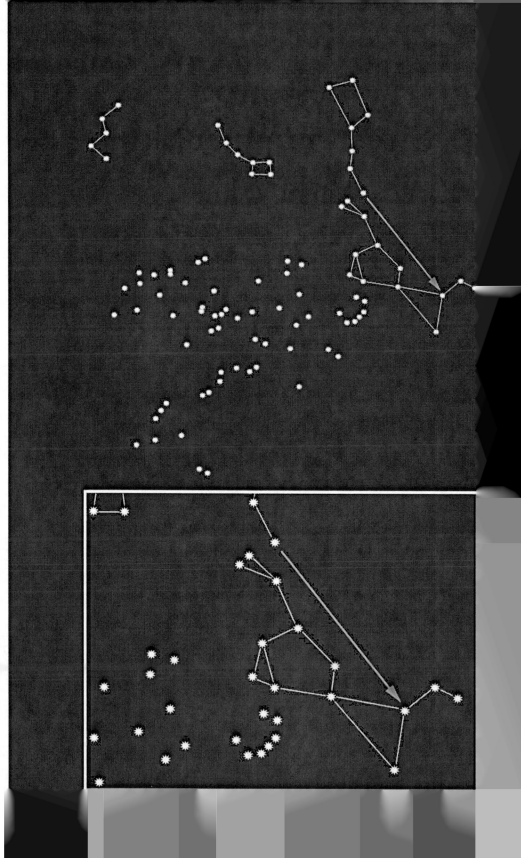

Boötes, the Herdsman

The Herdsman, Boötes (boo-OH-tees), contains one of my favorite stars to find. It's another red star, called Arcturus (arc-TER-us).

Find it using the Big Dipper; follow the arc of the handle to get to Arcturus. That red star is the brightest one you'll find in Boötes.

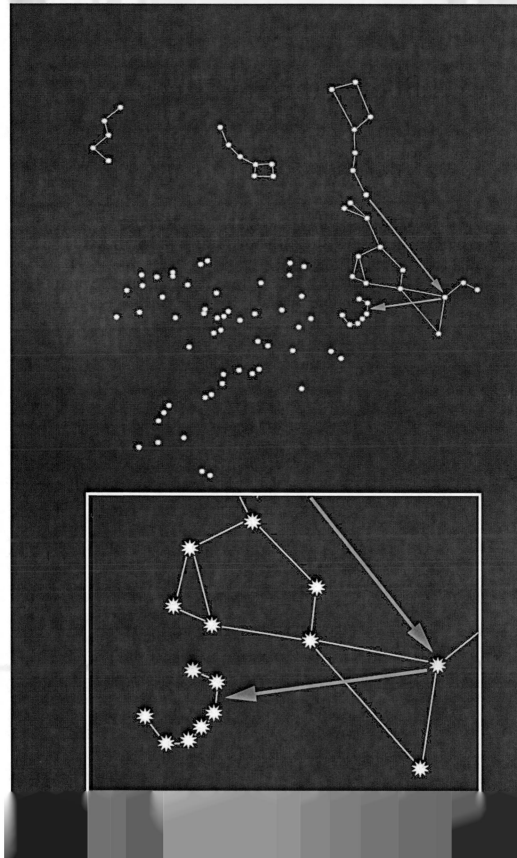

Corona Borealis,
the Northern Crown

I usually just call this one "Corona" because Corona Australis, the Southern Crown can't be seen in the northern hemisphere.

Find Corona by rolling an imaginary bouncy ball off the handle of the Big Dipper. The ball will hit Arcturus, and then bounce back up to land in Corona.

Corona forms a "C" shape (C is for Corona, or C is for Crown, take your pick), and it is oriented like a cup to catch the bouncy ball.

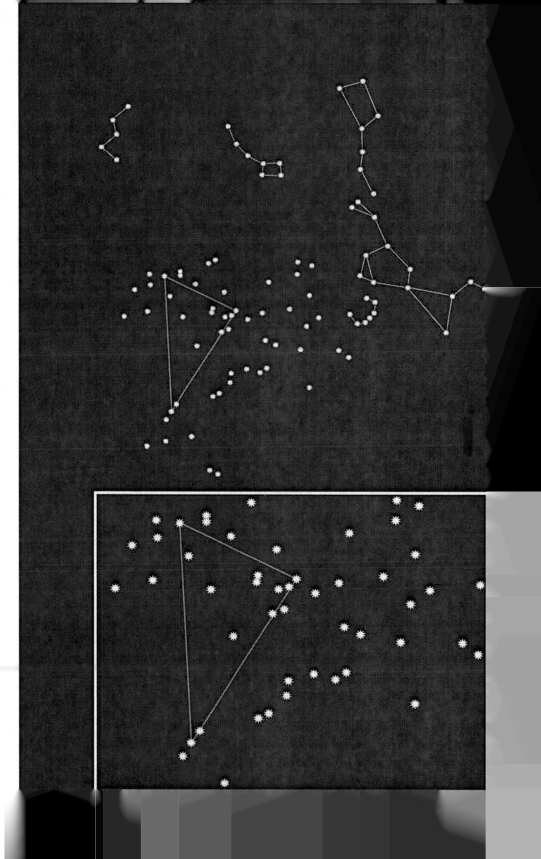

The Summer Triangle

A well-known asterism, the Summer Triangle is actually 3 bright stars from 3 different constellations.

To find this one, widen your gaze a bit. The Summer Triangle is quite large. Find 3 bright stars high overhead that form a triangle the same shape as the one shown to the left (in the middle of the summer at prime star-watching time, it's pretty much directly above you).

For orientation purposes, notice that the skinny end points away from the line formed by connecting the Big Dipper, the Little Dipper, and Cassiopeia.

Remember that in my diagrams, there are no distinctions between bright stars and faint stars. The points of the Summer Triangle in the real sky will be brighter than anything else around them; those three stars are the 5th (Vega), 12th (Altair), and 19th (Deneb) brightest stars in our night sky. It should be fairly easy to pick them out.

(Other stars in the top 20 we've already learned about: Sirius, Arcturus, Rigel, Procyon, Betelgeuse, Aldebaran, and Pollux).

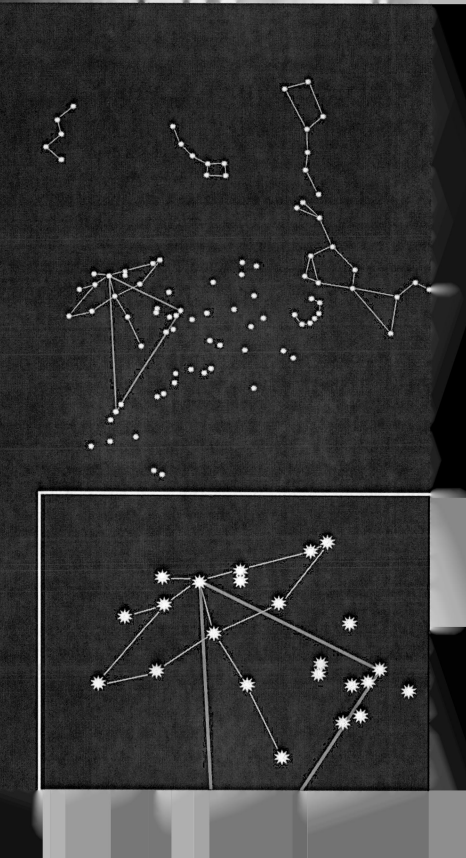

Cygnus, the Swan

The point of the Summer Triangle closest to Cassiopeia is the star Deneb, in the constellation Cygnus (SIG-nus).

Deneb is the tail of the swan, and the swan flies toward the triangle. An asterism within the swan is the Northern Cross.

The Southern Cross, visible in the southern hemisphere, "points" south the same way our Big Dipper "points" north.

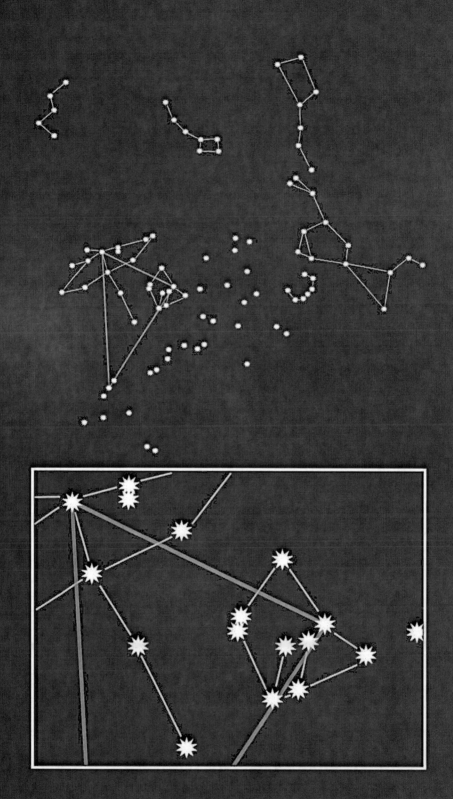

Lyra, the Lyre

Completing the short side of the Summer Triangle is the star Vega (VAY-guh), in the constellation Lyra (LEE-rah).

A Lyre is a stringed musical instrument, kind of like a harp.

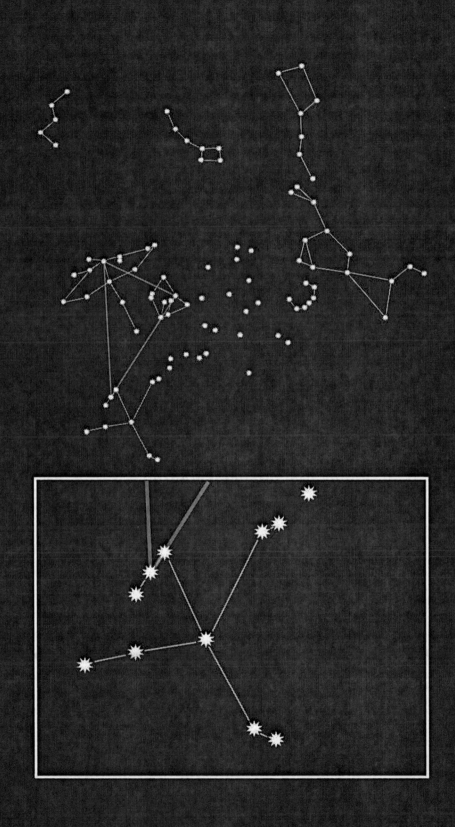

Aquila, the Eagle

Completing our Summer Triangle is the star Altair (ahl-TARE), in the constellation Aquila (uh-KWIL-uh).

Altair is one of the stars in the head of the eagle, and the beak of the eagle faces away from the triangle.

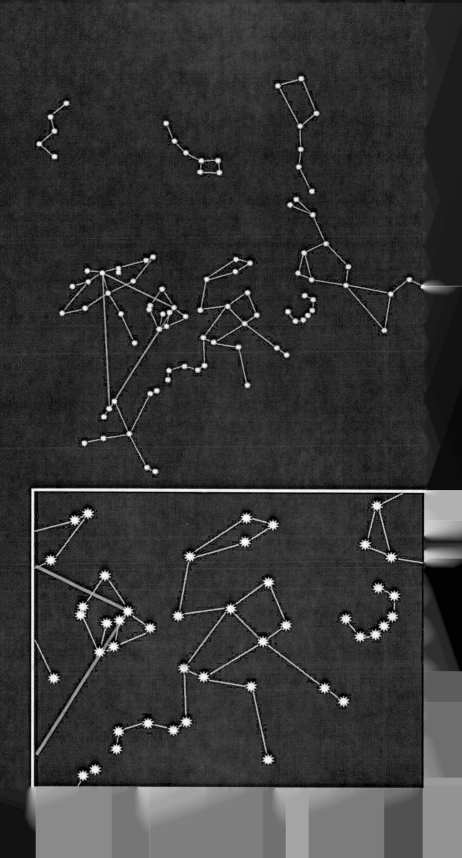

Hercules, the Hero

Nestled between Corona and the Summer Triangle is Hercules (HER-kyoo-leez). He holds a club above his head, and runs across the summer sky.

Hercules can be tricky to discern, as he is composed of faint stars, but once you can narrow down the region of sky by finding Corona and the Summer Triangle, you might as well see if you can pick him out.

The Milky Way

If you're in a really dark area, with no moon, and far away from city lights, the Milky Way will be easy to find. Otherwise, knowing exactly where to look can help you out.

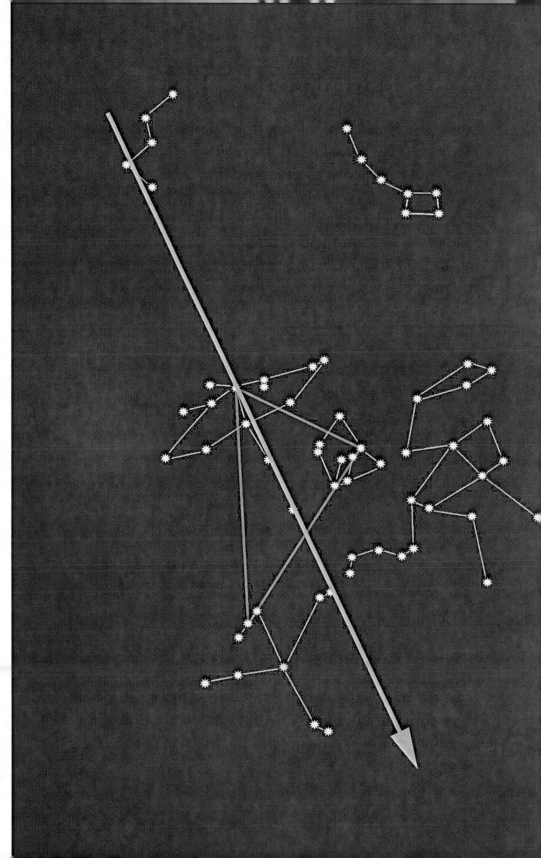

The Milky Way runs through Cassiopeia and Cygnus. If you can see those two constellations, look carefully and see if you can find it. The Milky Way is our galaxy, and you're seeing it from the inside. Our galaxy is shaped like a giant Frisbee in space.

Imagine you are a tiny ant wandering through a Frisbee factory. Suddenly, you fall into a vat of clear-blue molten plastic, and you get manufactured into a Frisbee. When you look up through of the top of the Frisbee, you can see a few molecules of clear blue plastic (stars) before you see the outside world (space). If you look down through the bottom of the Frisbee, you can also see a few molecules of plastic before you see the outside world. If, however, you try to look sideways through the Frisbee, there's so much plastic in the way, that all you see is bluish plastic.

When you see the Milky Way in the sky, it looks like a dense stripe of stars—you're looking sideways through the disk of the galaxy from inside it!

The term "Milky Way" comes from the Greek word for "galaxy" (galaxy = galactic = lactic = lactose = milk, right? Not quite, but following the etymology of the word from Hellenistic Greek, through Classical Latin, and on to English gets pretty close to that). With enough visible stars, the Milky Way certainly looks like someone spilled milk across the sky.

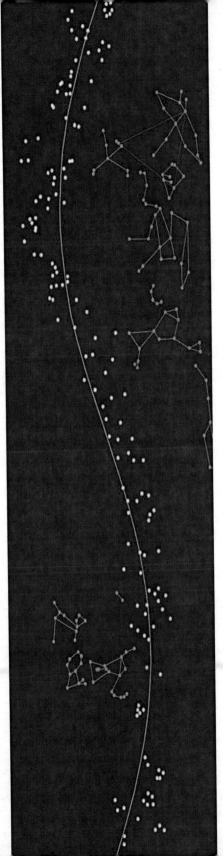

Lesson 6: The Zodiac Constellations

Why Are the Zodiac Constellations Significant?

The Zodiac Constellations are a group of 12 constellations that fall on either side of the ecliptic.

The ecliptic is the path that the sun traces through the sky, from the perspective of Earth, throughout the year.

Put another way, if you were to take a giant celestial crayon and draw a line through all 12 Zodiac Constellations, you would end up drawing a ring in the sky that goes all the way around the Earth.

The sun would always be near that ring, as would all of the planets (not Pluto, though... add that to the ever-lengthening list of reasons Pluto has been reclassified as a Dwarf Planet).

To the left, you'll see the ecliptic in dark grey, with the associated constellations. I have added other constellations we have learned so far, so you can get your bearings. The bottom part of the Big Dipper is just peeking through on the right-hand side of the picture in the center.

This picture shows the entire ecliptic, but since this line is really a circle with the Earth in the middle, you will only be able to see some if it at any given time.

At all times, there is a straight line that can be drawn from a Zodiac Constellation, through the sun, to the Earth. Over the course of a year as the Earth travels around the sun, each of the 12 Zodiac Constellations falls into this position lined up with the sun and the Earth in turn.

We'll go through each of the 12 Zodiac Constellations, traveling to the "left" along the ecliptic as we go. Some Zodiac Constellations can be found using other constellations we've learned about previously, but the rest you may just have to learn to find on your own.

When you're stargazing, if you can find any two Zodiac Constellations, you know that the ecliptic goes through them and continues on either side. Use that knowledge to find any others that might be visible at that moment.

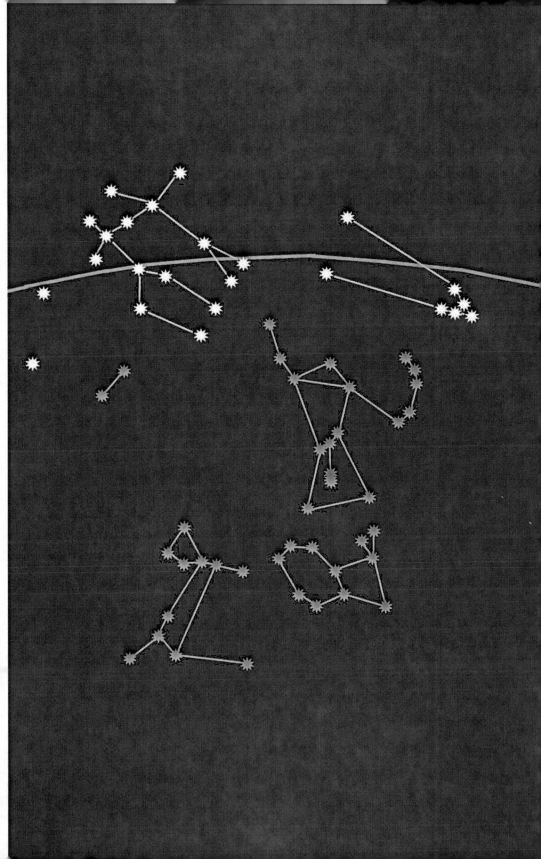

Taurus and Gemini

We're already familiar with both Taurus and Gemini.

Remember, you can use Orion's belt: follow the belt up and to the right to find Taurus's nose.

Now find Rigel (Orion's ankle) and Betelgeuse (Orion's opposite shoulder), and connect them. Continue up to find Gemini.

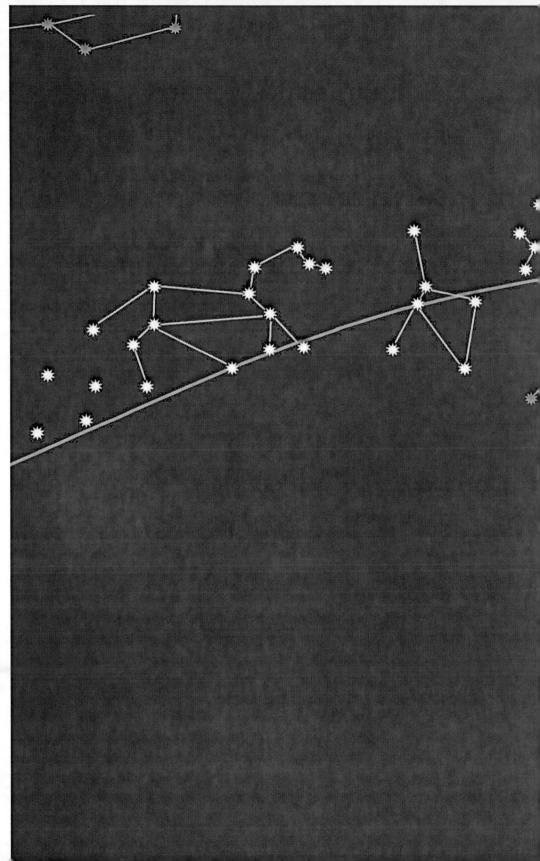

Cancer and Leo

Next to Gemini, you'll find Cancer, the crab. The wonky trapezoid is the body of the crab, and the two lines protruding outward are the claws.

The stars in Cancer are very faint, so he'll be difficult to see most nights. The easiest way to find him is to find Gemini and Leo, and then look between them.

Leo is a lion, and he faces toward Cancer. Leo's head, neck, and front left foot form a distinct backward question mark shape. That shape will be your key to finding Leo in the sky. Those stars are brighter than the rest of Leo.

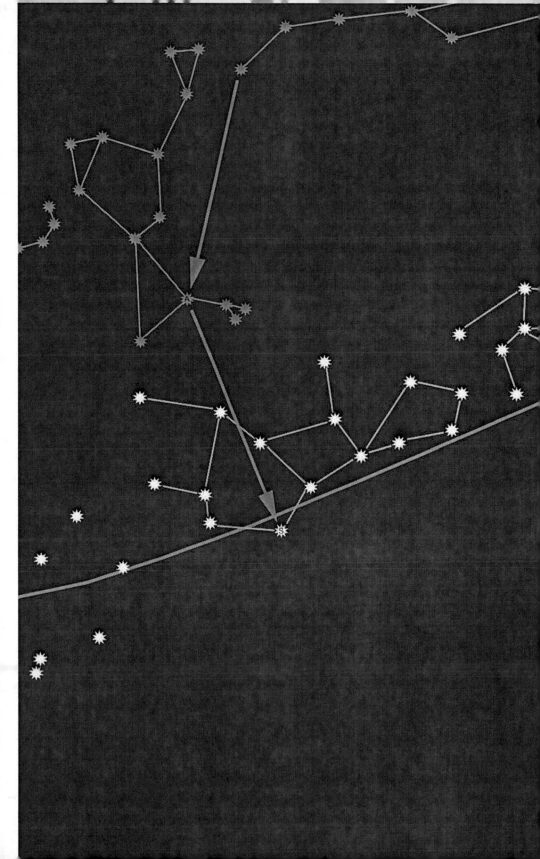

Virgo, the Virgin

Find the handle of the big dipper, and follow the arc to the red star, Arcturus. This time, instead of bouncing back up to Corona Borealis, "spike down" to a blue star, Spica (SPAI-kuh).

Spica is a fairly bright star, and is the only bright star in Virgo. Frequently, you'll be able to find Spica, and be unable to find any other stars in Virgo.

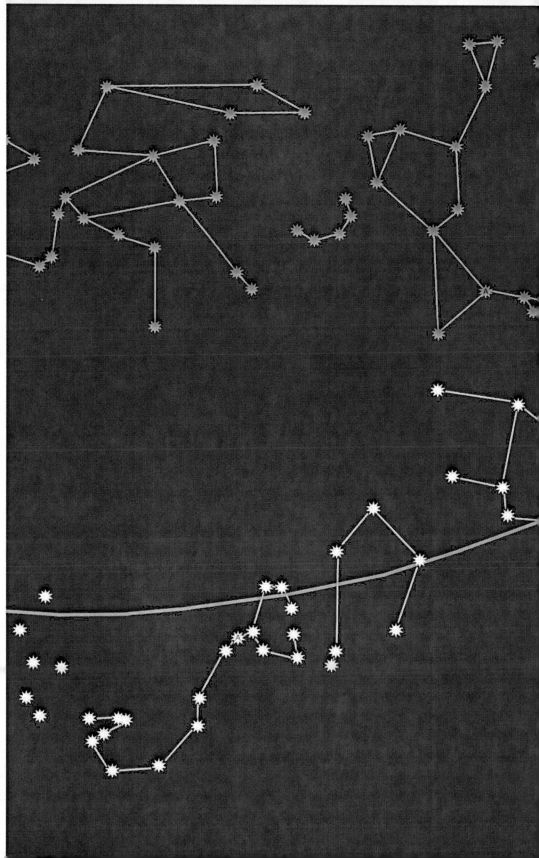

Libra and Scorpius

Libra, the scales, is the only non-living object represented by the Zodiac. The scales are usually depicted as those old-fashioned two-sided balances. This version is one side of the balance.

Scorpius, the scorpion, has a red star right at its heart, called Antares (an-TAHR-ees). The Milky Way goes through Scorpius, as well as through Cygnus and Cassiopeia.

Follow the path from Cassiopeia, through Cygnus, and onward until you find the red star. It will be low to the horizon in the summer.

Orion and Scorpius are enemies. According to the ancient Greeks, the gods put Scorpius and Orion as far away from each other in the sky as possible. If you can see Scorpius, Orion is below the horizon 180° away, and vice versa.

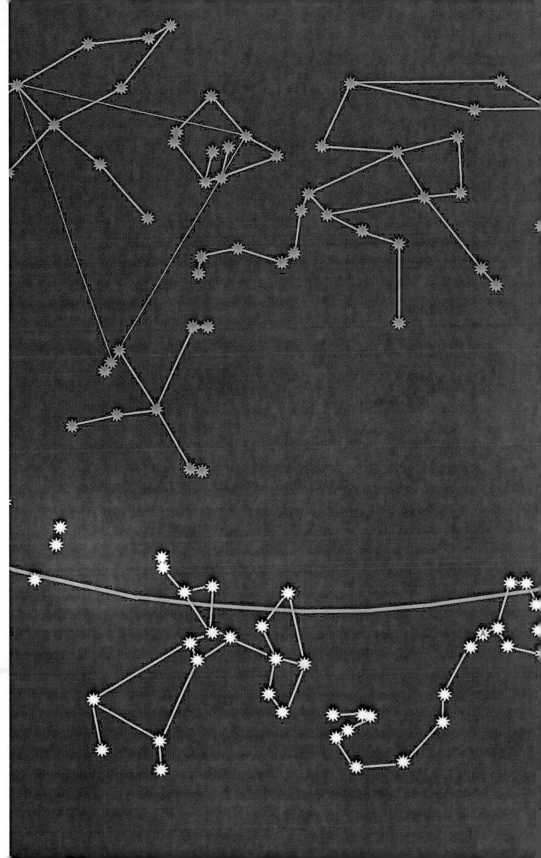

Sagittarius, the Archer

The archer aims his bow and shoots his arrow toward Scorpius. Sagittarius also appears very low to the horizon in the northern hemisphere, so it may be difficult to see him most of the time.

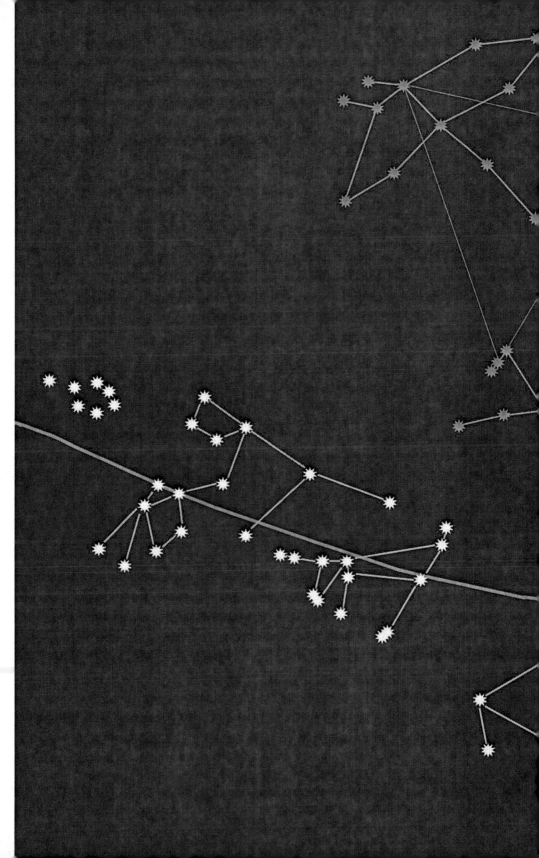

Capricorn and Aquarius

In this depiction, Capricorn, the goat, is leaning down to eat some grass near his feet, with his tail in the air, and horns pointed toward Aquarius. Following the point of the Summer Triangle through Altair may be helpful in finding Capricorn's tail.

Aquarius, the water bearer, is leaping over Capricorn, and water is spilling out of the bucket that he bears (see what happens when you run with a full bucket of water?)

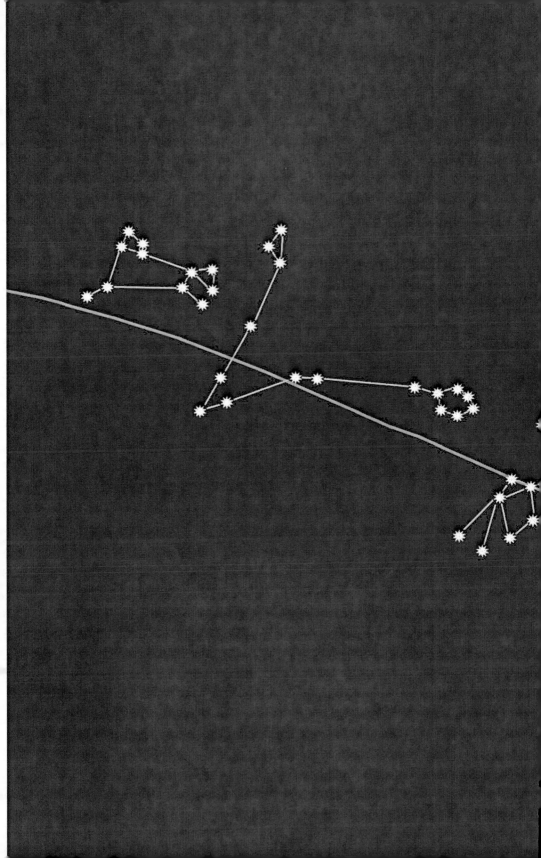

Pisces and Aries

Pisces is two fish with their tails tied together. The "V" shape is the rope that holds them together, and the circle and triangle at the ends of the rope are the fish.

Aries, the ram, leaps toward the rope in Pisces, and away from Taurus (we've come all the way around again).

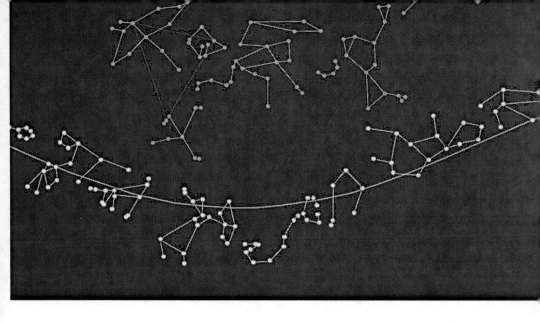

The Duodecuple Zodiac

The diagram to the right shows the relationship between the orbit of the Earth and the Zodiac Constellations. As the Earth makes its way around the sun over the course of a year, it lines up with different Zodiac constellations.

When the sun is "up," so is a corresponding constellation (but, of course you can't see it because it's daytime). Exactly one month later, a different Zodiac Constellation will be "behind" the sun during the daytime. The diagram shows two examples and their corresponding dates, and you can extrapolate the remainder of the dates from there.

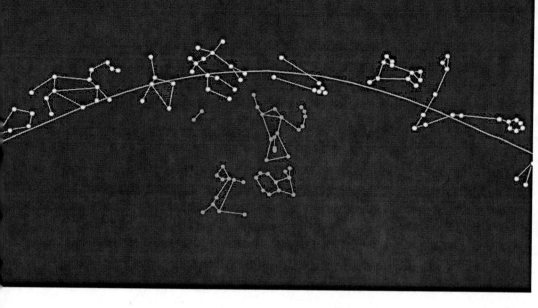

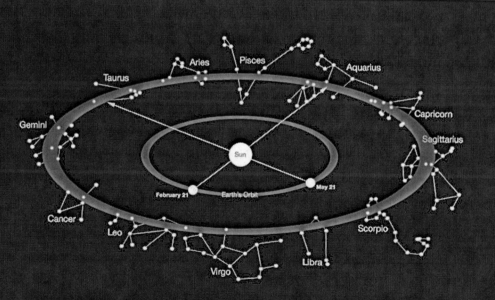

On February 21st, the Earth and sun are in line with Aquarius. This means that on the side of Earth that Faces away from the sun (when it's dark), Aquarius cannot be seen, but Leo should be quite visible. On May 21st, the sun is directly between the Earth and Taurus, and Scorpio becomes visible at night.

Further Study

Impress Your Friends

You have now mastered 27 constellations and a few asterisms visible in the northern hemisphere. That's 30% of the 88 modern constellations, but as you stargaze in the northern hemisphere, you'll find that you can now identify 70-80% of the sky you can see at any given time. Many of the other northern hemisphere constellations are comparatively small or faint.

If you still find a patch of sky you can't quite figure out, look it up. Now that you know most of the constellations, looking at a star chart won't be quite as intimidating.

Are you seeing a bright star that doesn't seem to fit what you know about the nearby constellations? Is it near a Zodiac Constellation? It's probably a planet!

Look for These

Some constellations that we haven't covered are worth noting:

Andromeda and Pegasus share a star (well, not technically, but close enough), and can be seen late in the evening in the summer. Pegasus's wings form a gigantic square of bright stars, which seem to dominate that part of the sky. Andromeda contains within it the Andromeda Galaxy, or Messier 31. Approximately 2.6 million light years away, this galaxy is one of the most distant objects that can be seen from Earth with the naked eye.

Perseus is another good one to know how to find. Mid-August each year brings with it the Perseid (PER-see-id) meteor showers, or Perseids. Meteors are "shooting stars" or "falling stars," but they're not really stars at all. These streaks of light across the sky are actually bits of rock, dust, particles, and space debris burning as they enter Earth's upper atmosphere.

The debris that causes the Perseids comes from the Swift-Tuttle comet. Check local reference materials for when Perseus will be highest in the sky during the Perseids, grab a sleeping bag and a portable alarm clock (depending on the time) and get ready for a spectacular show!

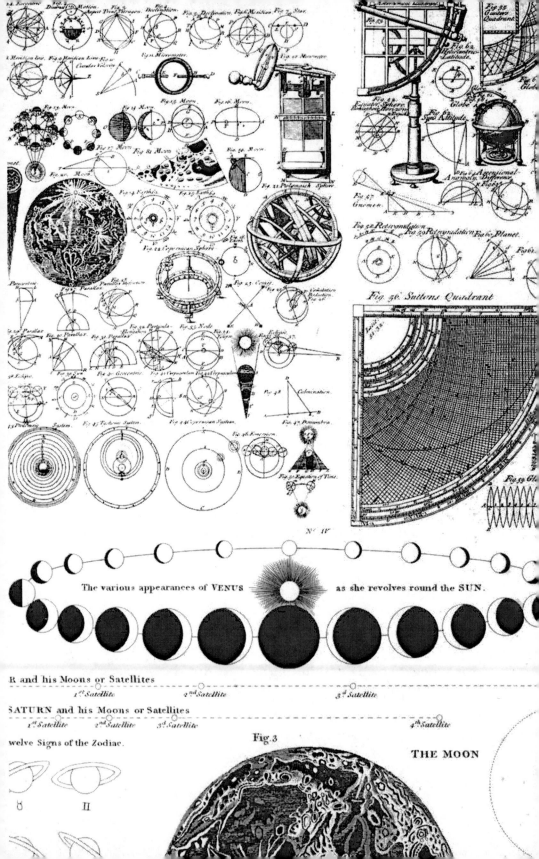

The various appearances of VENUS as she revolves round the SUN.

R and his Moons or Satellites

1st Satellite   2nd Satellite   3d Satellite

SATURN and his Moons or Satellites

1st Satellite   2nd Satellite   3d Satellite   4th Satellite

welve Signs of the Zodiac.

Fig. 3

THE MOON

Appendix A
Light Years

A light year is a measure of distance, not time; is the distance light can travel in one Earth year.

Distance light travels in one
second: 186,282 miles or 299,793 kilometers
minute: 11,176,920 miles or 17,987,580 kilometers
hour: 670,615,200 miles or 1,079,254,800 kilometers
day: 16,094,764,800 miles or 25,902,115,200 kilometers
year: 5,874,589,150,000 miles or 9,454,272,050,000 km

Distances in space are so large, that astronomers find it inconvenient to discuss them in miles or kilometers. The nearest star to Earth, other than our sun, is 4.4 light years away. Take that bottom number—the distance light travels in one year—and multiply it by 4.4 to get the distance to Alpha Centauri in miles or kilometers. That's just the closest star! A number like 4.4 is much more manageable to say, write, and think about.

Apparent Magnitude

The apparent magnitude of a star (or other celestial object) is a measure of its brightness, as seen by an observer on Earth. The number compensates for viewing the stars from Earth with no atmospheric interference.

Lower magnitudes indicate brighter stars; magnitudes higher than 6 are not visible with the naked eye. Each whole number is about 2.5 times brighter than one number higher (a star with an apparent magnitude of 2.0 is about two-and-a-half times brighter than a star with an apparent magnitude of 3.0).

Top 20 Brightest Stars

The table to the right shows the top 20 brightest stars in order of apparent magnitude, along with a few more important ones previously discussed in this book. Distance from Earth is given in light years.

	Apparent Magnitude	Star Name	Constellation	Distance in Light Years
0	-26.74	Sun		0.000016
1	-1.46	Sirius	Canis Major	8.6
2	-0.72	Canopus	Carina	310
3	-0.04	Arcturus	Boötes	37
4	-0.01	Alpha Centauri	Centaurus	4.4
5	0.03	Vega	Lyra	25
6	0.12	Rigel	Orion	770
7	0.34	Procyon	Canis Minor	11
8	0.42	Betelgeuse	Orion	640
9	0.50	Achernar	Eridanus	140
10	0.60	Beta Centauri	Centaurus	530
11	0.71	Capella A	Auriga	43
12	0.77	Altair	Aquila	17
13	0.85	Aldebaran	Taurus	65
14	0.96	Capella B	Auriga	42
15	1.04	Spica	Virgo	260
16	1.09	Antares	Scorpius	600
17	1.15	Pollux	Gemini	34
18	1.16	Fomalhaut	Piscis Austrinus	25
19	1.25	Deneb	Cygnus	1550
20	1.30	Beta Crucis	Crux	350
22	1.35	Regulus	Leo	77
27	1.64	Bellatrix	Orion	240
44	1.96	Castor A	Gemini	52
45	1.97	Polaris	Ursa Minor	430
70	2.27	Mizar	Ursa Major	78

Appendix B

Planets

The word planet comes from the Greek for "wandering star." Before the motion of celestial bodies was fully understood, some celestial bodies appeared to be "fixed" and some appeared to "wander" about the sky. Stars are so far away from us, that from our perspective here on Earth, they stay in the same positions relative to each other. Planets on the other hand, are much closer and can move independently of the starry background.

Think about driving past a picket fence with a mountain in the distance. The fence posts appear to move quickly, and the mountain moves not at all. That is because the fence is very close, so compared to far away objects it appears to move. The Greeks saw the stars staying put (relative to each other) and the wanderers moved. They moved in predictable ways and along determined paths, but still they moved.

Planets can be found near they ecliptic (where you'll find all the Zodiac Constellations). If you're stargazing, and you notice a bright object that looks like a star, but isn't in the correct place for that constellation, you're probably looking at a planet. Consult charts of planetary locations for the date in question to determine which planet it is.

If you've heard that you can tell the difference between stars and planets easily because planets don't twinkle, you've heard a popular myth. Twinkling is caused by atmospheric distortion, and although it's more common for this to occur with point sources of light rather than reflected light (stars are light sources, planets simply reflect light from the sun), sometimes it also happens to planets, and sometimes it doesn't happen to stars. You can also trick your eyes into believing what you want them to when you're dealing with tiny bits of light in the dark. Stare at a star. Convince yourself that it is not twinkling. You'll probably see it stop twinkling. Now tell yourself that it is twinkling. Watch it twinkle.

All Things Are Connected

In ancient times, only the celestial bodies closest to the Earth in our Solar System were known. Everything beyond Saturn was too far away and too small to be seen, but the closer objects were studied carefully. Long before humans accurately understood how celestial bodies moved in relation to each other, we could discern how they moved in relation to us.

One observable characteristic is the speed of celestial objects as perceived from Earth. The celestial objects in our Solar System in order of speed are as follows: Moon, Mercury, Venus, Sun, Mars, Jupiter, Saturn. You may have noticed that the days of the week come from the names of celestial bodies, but did you ever wonder why they are in that order?

The Sun and the Moon were the "nearest" and most important objects in the sky (although Mercury and Venus are closer than the sun, the sun appears larger in our sky because its absolute size is so much greater than any planet). The Sun and the Moon were awarded the first two days of the week.

Each planet that came after the Sun and Moon in the sequence were seen as descending in order of importance, and the days were arranged accordingly, alternating between the Sun and Moon. It helps to think of it like two separate lists, and the Sun and Moon are team captains.

The full list, in order: Moon Mercury, Venus, Sun, Mars, Jupiter, Saturn.

Moon   Sun
Mercury   Mars
Venus   Jupiter
          Saturn

Sun comes first.	(Sunday, Solis, Domingo, Sól)
Then Moon.	(Monday, Lūnae, Lunes, Máni)
Back to Sun's list: Mars.	(Tuesday, Martis, Martes, Tyr)
Back to Moon: Mercury.	(Wednesday, Mercurii, Miércoles, Odin)
Switch again: Jupiter.	(Thursday, Jovis, Jueves, Thor)
Back again: Venus.	(Friday, Veneris, Viernes, Frigg)
And finally, Saturn.	(Saturday, Saturni, Sábado, Saturn)

Thus, the order of the days of the week was determined.

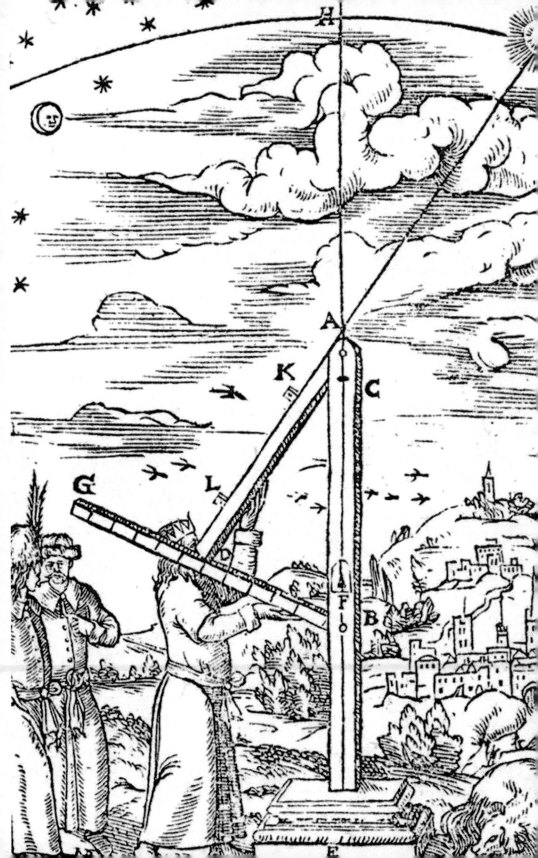

Appendix C
Star Charts

Star charts can be useful when looking for a particular constellation, or for identifying one you see in the field. The following star charts are centered on a particular constellation, and show relative brightness and apparent magnitude of stars (see Appendix A), as well as other astronomical points of interest.

Though the lines connecting the stars may be different than what you have seen earlier in this book, the stars themselves will be the same. Differently drawn lines are to be expected, as it seems every astronomy reference has its own nuance to connecting the dots.

The star charts on the following pages are from IAU and Sky & Telescope magazine (Roger Sinnott & Rick Fienberg), used under the terms of the Creative Commons 3.0 Attribution Unported license.

Andromeda

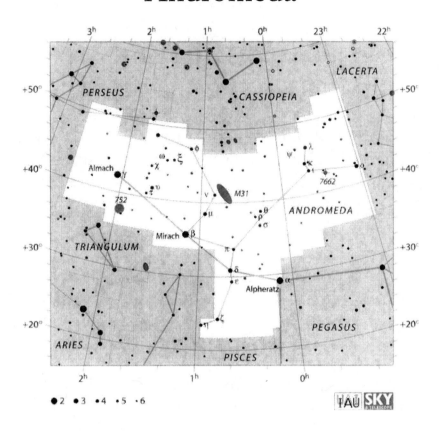

Aquarius

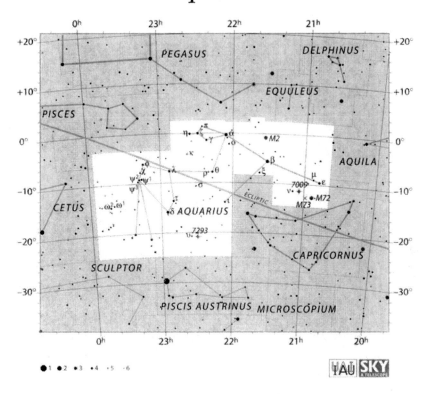

Aquila

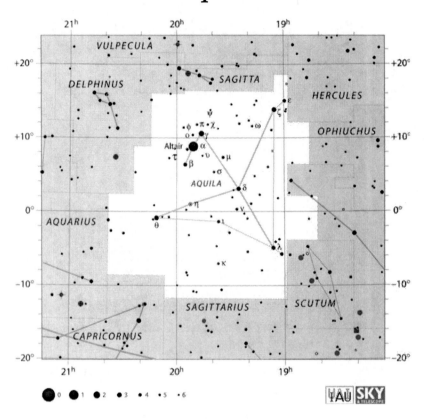

Aries

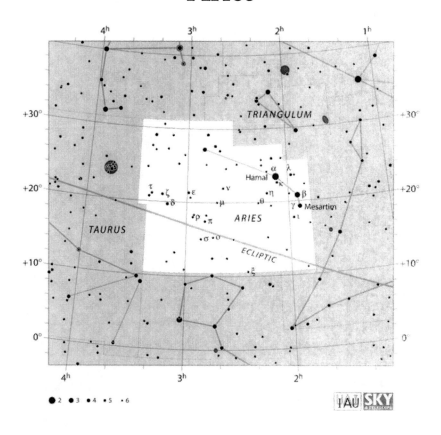

Boötes

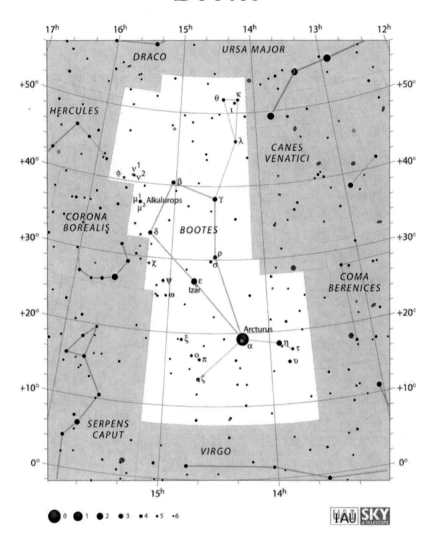

Cancer

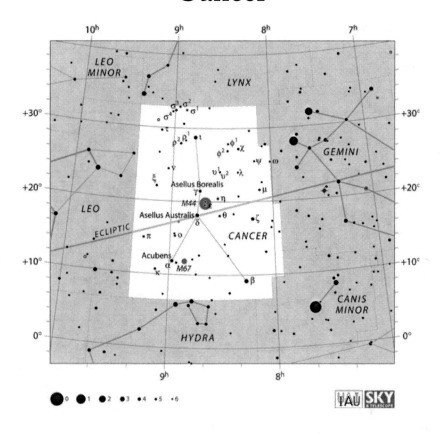

Canis Major

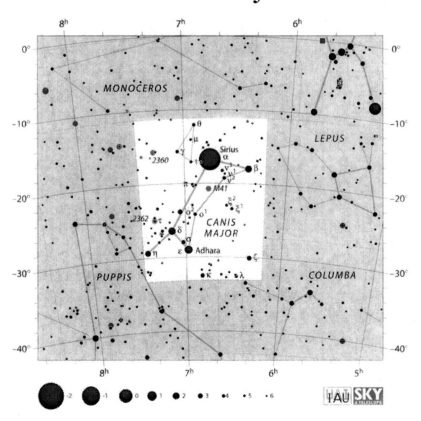

Canis Minor

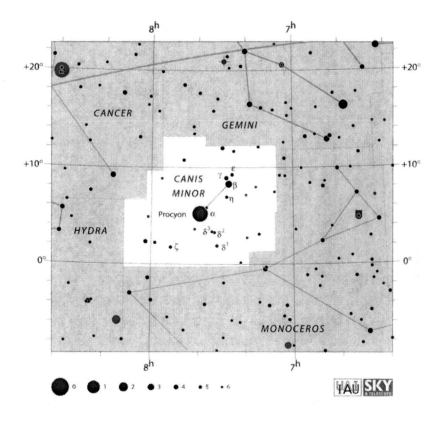

Capricornus

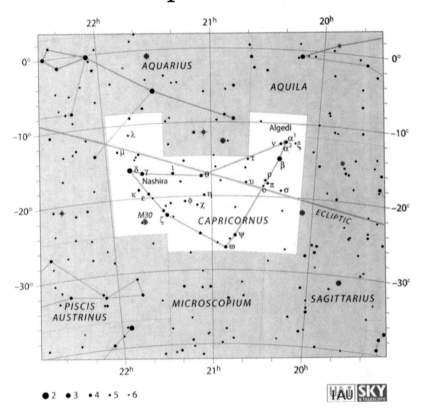

Cassiopeia

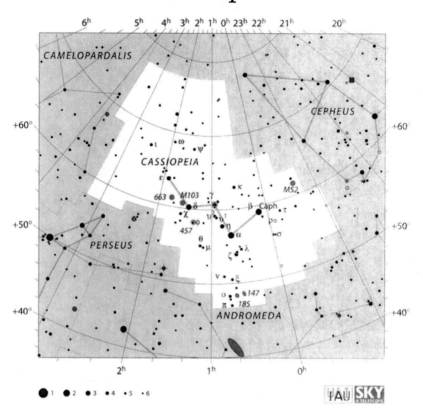

Cepheus

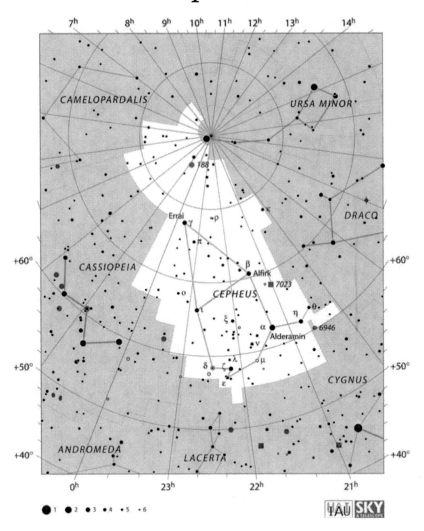

Corona Borealis

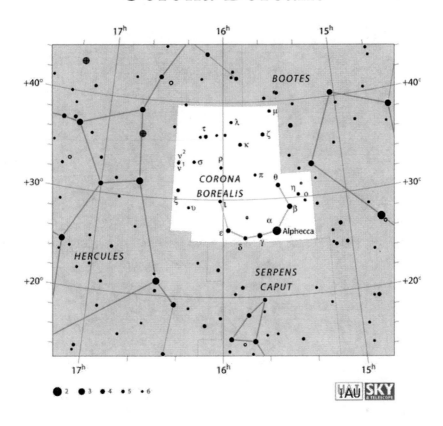

Cygnus

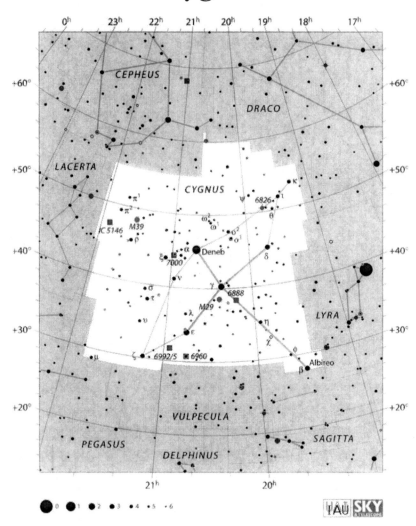

Draco

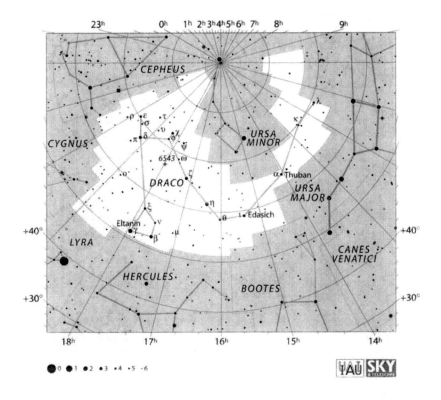

Gemini

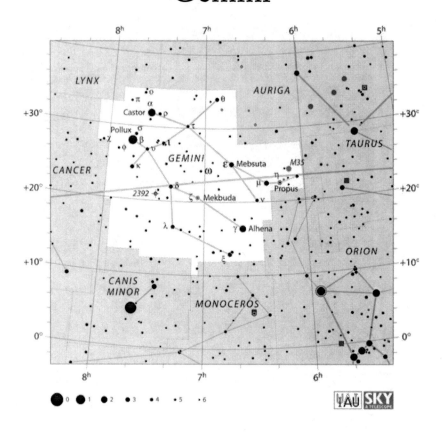

Hercules

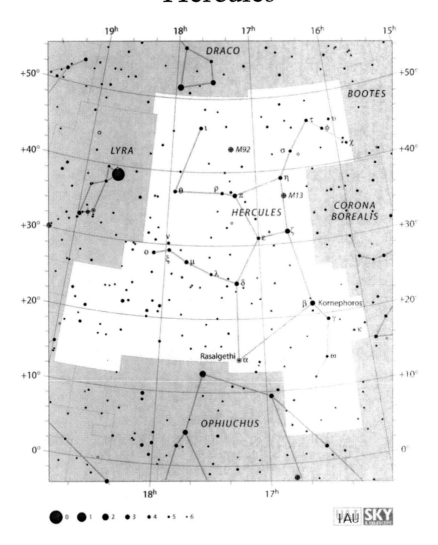

Leo

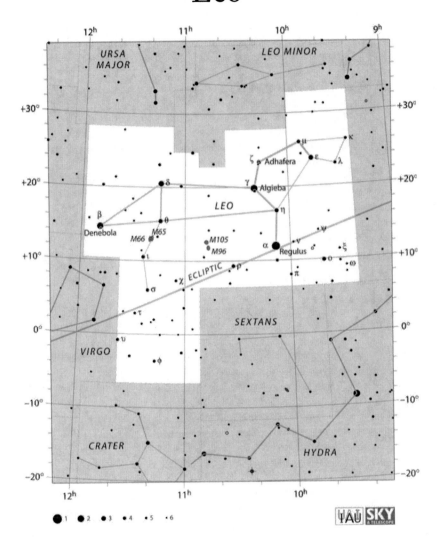

Lepus

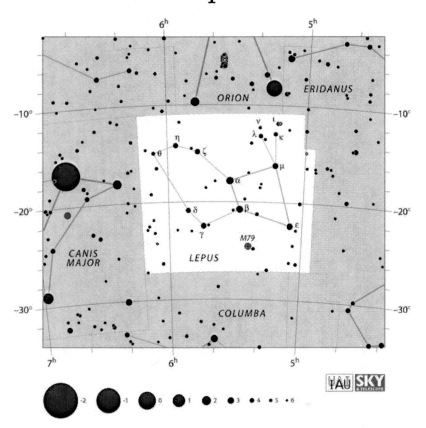

Libra

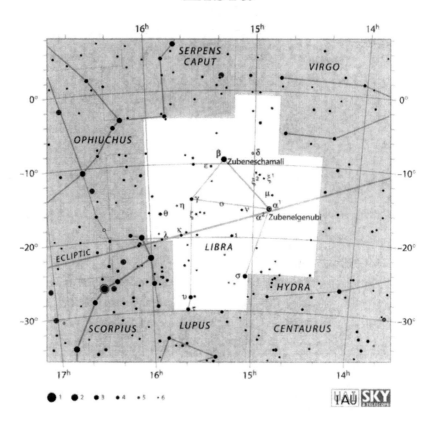

Lyra

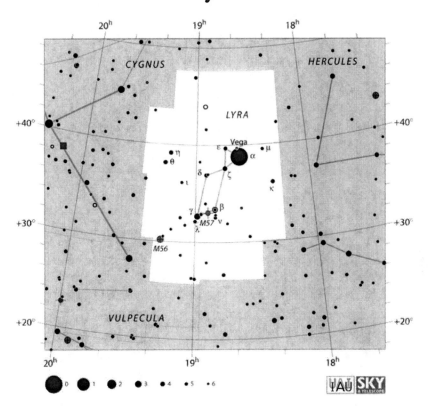

Orion

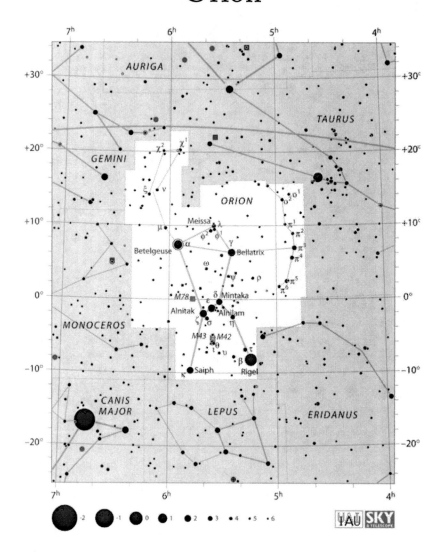

Pegasus

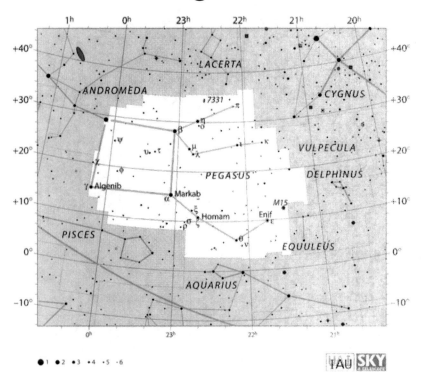

● 1 ● 2 ● 3 • 4 · 5 · 6

Perseus

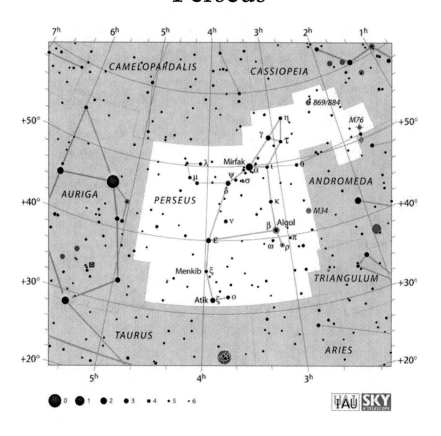

Pisces

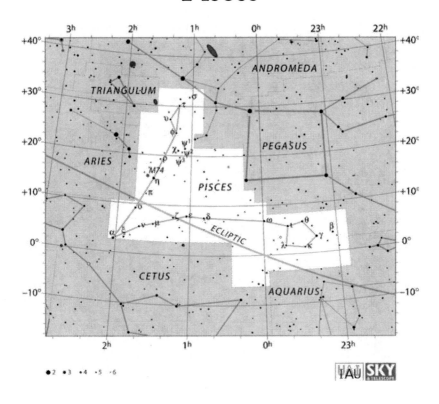

Sagittarius

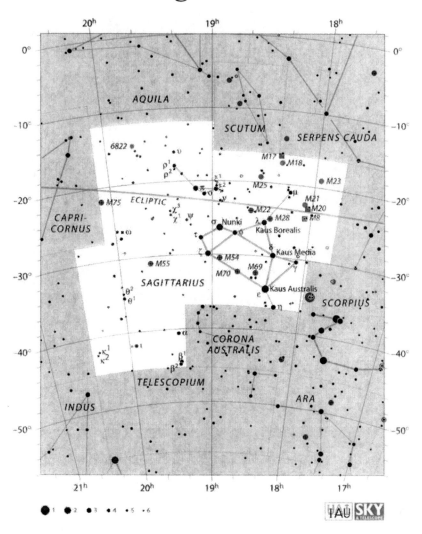

Scorpius

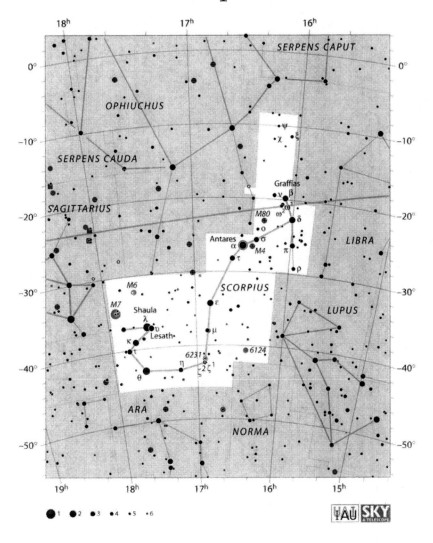

Taurus and The Pleiades

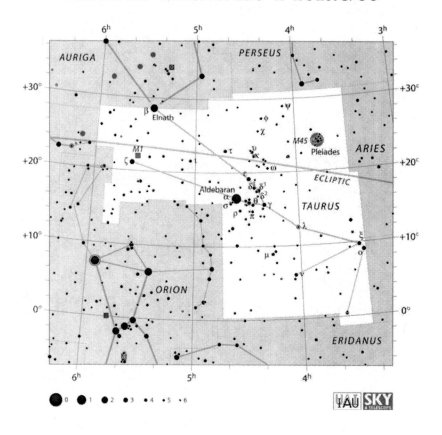

Ursa Major

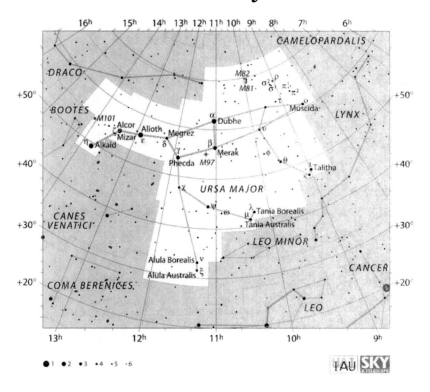

Ursa Minor

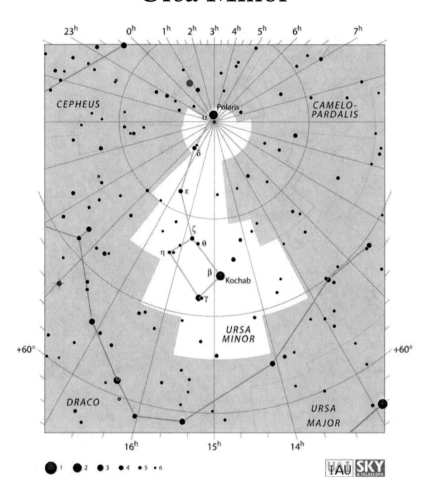

Virgo

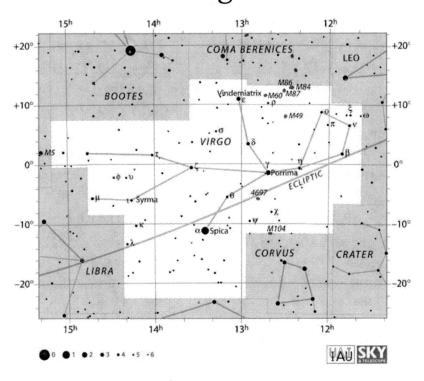

Index

Idle
Winter
Press